NAN BERRIAN

Vows, Wows, and WTF?!

HOW I FOUND MY VOICE AND REWROTE MY LIFE AFTER "I DO" FELL APART

SHINE
PRESS

SHINE
— P R E S S —

Publisher: Shine Press
4522 W. Village Dr. #1294
Tampa, Florida 34624
Shine-Press.com | Jodi@Shine-Press.com
Shine Press is an imprint of Jodi K Costa, LLC.

Disclaimer: This book is a personal account of my experiences and perspective. The events, conversations, and situations described are based on my own life, and while I have made every effort to present them as accurately as possible, they are filtered through my personal lens.

Please note that some names and other identifying details may have been changed to protect the privacy of individuals mentioned in this story.

For speaking engagements, event invitations, bulk orders, and other author requests, please contact her publisher: Jodi@Shine-Press.com

AUTHOR PHOTOGRAPHY CREDIT: Rich Berrian

FIRST EDITION

ISBN: 979-8-9993665-1-1
Ebook also available

Shine Press offers writing, editing, designing, publishing, and marketing services, focusing on high quality at affordable prices with an excellent author experience.

Contact us for more information about our personalized Spark Books, publishing packages, book marketing, and Bestseller Campaign.

The first person I am dedicating this book to is my smart and beautiful daughter. All the challenges you have faced have empowered you to create an inner strength that will only grow stronger over time. I am very proud of who you are and who you are becoming. I know you are on your own path, but I hope my story and my lessons will also help guide you. I love you, kiddo, with all my heart and soul. You are the girl I wish I could have been, and you deserve the best the world has to offer you.

This book was also written for those who have been silenced for whatever reason—it is your time to speak.

"It took me quite a long time to develop a voice, and now that I have it, I am not going to be silent."
Madeleine Albright

Contents

Prologue

When I was young, I wanted to be J. Lo before there was a J. Lo. I dreamed of being a triple-threat entertainer—singing, dancing, and acting. It's kinda funny when I think about it now, because I truly *dislike* people staring at me. Case in point: I started to hyperventilate on my wedding day just getting ready to walk down the aisle. (Although that may have been for a totally different reason.)

But when I was on stage—singing someone else's lyrics, speaking someone else's lines, dancing to someone else's choreography—I felt confident and at ease. It was the *real* me, Nancy Elaine Berrian, that I struggled to show. Being seen as *myself* felt raw, uncomfortable... even painful, at times.

So why the hell would I pour my heart out in a book?

Because I want to reach anyone who's ever felt like they lost themselves—or their voice—and let them know they're not alone. And maybe give you a few laughs along the way... at my expense!

In grade school, while dreaming of being a starlet, I learned about the artist Grandma Moses, who became popular in her golden years. I desperately didn't want that to be my fate—because I was going to be famous sooner rather than later! For what? I didn't know. I just was. I felt it in my bones.

But the acting/dancing/singing didn't work out—mostly because I didn't have the drive to pursue it. And, let's be honest, I wasn't Jenny from the Block. I was Nancy from the suburbs. So, I gave up on that dream.

Yet here I am, writing a book at 60. Not expecting any fame, but finally putting myself out there. Go figure.

This part of my life story focuses on my 26-year marriage, subsequent divorce, and ultimate triumph. Yes, I said it—*triumph*—because it's true. I've triumphed over some of life's hardest moments, and you can too.

I know that because earlier in life, I never would've had the confidence—or belief—that I had it in me to really, truly conquer any adversity. But guess what? We *all* do. And I want you to remember that as you read what I'm about to share.

This is my story. But I'm sure parts of it will resonate with you. Maybe not the details—some of them are pretty bizarre!—but hopefully the feelings I'm trying to convey will strike a chord.

Now, don't get me wrong: I know I'm not unique. As my oldest sister, Diane, kindly pointed out when I told her I wanted to share my prose with the world: "Who would want to read *your* story anyway?"

Fair question.

My answer? It's for anyone who has ever felt silenced—by family, marriage, politics, society, work… whatever it may be. If that's you, then this is for you.

Know that you can find yourself—and your voice—again. If not today, then someday.

Also, there are two sides to every story in a marriage, right? Well, this is my side of things—my narrative about what happened at the start of my divorce and the sometimes anxiety-ridden, but still fun-filled, adventurous journey that followed. I'm an open book, so you can be damn sure I'll be sharing my mistakes and imperfections along the way. But just to be clear: everything I'm writing is based on my perception of what happened. Nothing is embellished—not even my reactions.

It's taken me five years to write this, and I'm finally ready for you to come along for the ride. So let's begin. Strap in—it's going to be a bumpy one!

Imagine you've been married for 26 years. Things have been rough on and off, and for the past four years, you and your spouse have been sleeping in separate rooms—for all the wrong reasons. As a tradition-al wife raised Catholic, you believe in "good times and bad" and are limping along, hoping something will change. You've tried your hardest to make it work, but you're stuck. You don't know where to turn or how to fix it.

Apparently, your husband has other ideas—and decides to share them with you two days before your son's high school graduation.

This is how it all began.

1

There's Something I Need to Tell You

One day, I was sitting on my back porch enjoying a beautiful, warm June day. My son, who was diagnosed with Asperger's syndrome (Autism Spectrum Disorder, or ASD) during his sophomore year, was about to graduate from high school. He and his sister had both struggled with school, so as a family, we agreed he should try attending our local community college to see how he would do. I had a lot of anxiety about whether he could handle it, but the warm sun really helped my mood.

My husband, L., who worked from home, joined me, and we talked a little bit about our son's plans. After some more small talk, he said:

"I've been thinking. I'm unhappy, you're unhappy. I want to see other people and I want a divorce."

He says it with almost a smile on his face and excited energy. Suddenly, my heart stops and everything inside freezes. But it's not just a cold feeling—it's more like my insides were being locked in steel. I could barely breathe. I felt sick. I would continue to feel that way, off and on, for three years. Especially any time I had to encounter him.

Getting back to my reaction: I was blindsided and shocked. Stunned. Yet somehow, I had the presence of mind to ask him, "Are you already seeing someone?"

His answer was yes.

Over the years, this man had sat in judgment of all others before him who had admitted to affairs and asked the same question: "How could they do that?" I clearly misunderstood indignation for what was probably directions or information. Mistakenly, as he was confessing to me, I thanked him for being honest. I didn't want to go through the same situation as others who had to find out about infidelity by accident.

Unfortunately for me, however, he took my acceptance as permission to tell me *everything* in detail—whether I wanted to know it or not.

To begin with, he explained that he had placed a profile on a dating website a few weeks before (or so he *claimed*—I later learned it had been going on for months) and was inundated with requests for dates. Intimidated by the response, he decided to take the profile down. But before he did, he got the contact information for three women and decided he would meet them for coffee.

Bachelorette #1 was a single mom of four children. She had already been married once and was on her second marriage, but claimed to be separated for three years. She told him her first husband embezzled money, which is why she left him, and said that her second husband "had issues." But husband #2 was a Navy veteran, and therefore, she couldn't afford to give up his benefits.

She managed a horse farm with the help of her father, and L. was clearly smitten by her because she was a "hard worker" and had long, curly hair. (Mine was short at the time due to an unfortunate style choice I made, and—yes—that bad choice was brought up to me during our separation.)

Plus, he liked that she "was a ball buster," meaning he thought she was tough. But he didn't appreciate how she also swore, which was one of his pet peeves. Eventually, I looked this woman up through Facebook since he had given me her name—wouldn't you? She is attractive, I'll give you that.

Bachelorette #2 didn't make the grade after their coffee date because when L. asked her what she did for a living, she said she "had been a prostitute." He told me he wasn't sure if she was kidding or not, so he decided not to pursue her. Thank goodness he had some scruples, right?

As for Bachelorette #3, he explained that he hadn't met her yet and was undecided about whether he would. More on her later.

During the week this *Ring of Hell* was happening, we talked about the dissolution of our relationship. He admitted he had learned dysfunctional behavior from his parents—such as, whenever they fought, his mother would say she was going to leave, but never did. Since that "pushing and pulling" felt normal to him, he finally realized he had used it frequently throughout our 26-year marriage.

Most notably was when he wanted sex. One minute he would be a complete jerk to me, or yelling about something, and then at night he would want us to be intimate. That didn't fly with me, and was one of the biggest reasons we were in separate rooms.

However, he said this time "was different" (with Bachelorette #1). He also recognized how he had put conditions on our relationship—expecting me to clean the way his mother did, to get a job that he approved of, to wear my hair the way he liked, etc.

(Fun fact: the reason my hair had been short over the years was due to a perm gone awry. He liked curly, 80s-style hair, and after three attempts by a professional stylist to get it right, it broke off.)

Even though his revelations were coming *now*, they were welcome to me because I had waited for the moment he would finally recognize what I already knew: that his adverse childhood experiences would never be resolved.

Back to his dates.

Bachelorette #1 was something of a dating coach, it turns out, and had suggested he should date multiple women. But when he did, she was upset by that. You would think this would be a clue about her personality, but as stated earlier, he was smitten—and therefore didn't see the signs of what was to come.

He was so attracted to her, in fact, that he brazenly texted her right in front of me. When I realized what he was doing, I asked if he would be moving out, because I did not want to put up with him carrying on like that in front of me.

His response cut through me like a Samurai sword.

He told me he was going to ask his lawyer what he should do when he saw him the next day.

I decided I needed to protect myself too, so I made an appointment to see a lawyer. I'm not sure why, but I still didn't want this divorce to happen. At the same time, I knew too many people who hadn't gotten good advice under circumstances like these, and I wanted to be careful—especially since he was acting irrationally.

A few days later, L. told me that his lawyer advised him *not* to move out, despite the fact that he was openly cheating. He also mentioned that the process could take as little as 60 to 90 days—about three months—if we chose mediation.

I tried to accept the situation as gracefully as possible. Even when, that Saturday, he told me he was "going out." Trying to sound casual, but dying on the inside, I joked, "With Bachelorette #1 or #3?"

He replied, "It's better that you don't know."

At first, I thought I could handle this. But as soon as he left the house, I knew I couldn't. I was shaking with rage.

So, I followed him. He said he was stopping at the store before his date. I planned to confront him then and there—or at the very least, let the air out of his tires. Whichever happened first.

Unfortunately, he wasn't in the parking lot. But as I drove away, we passed each other.

Just like in the movies, it was an "Oh shit!" moment.

Inevitably, he called and asked why I was there. I gave him an excuse—told him I had planned to buy something but changed my mind and was heading to my brother's house. Then I asked when he thought he'd be home.

He said, "I don't know."

Talk about a kick to the stomach.

Fighting my rage, I decided to let him know how I really felt. When I got to my brother's house, I texted him:

"I thought I was okay with this situation, but I am not. So, I respectfully request that you move out. If you do not, then I am just enabling you."

Enabling was one of his favorite words—usually lobbed at me when questioning my parenting. I figured it was time to use it on him.

He either didn't pick up on it or decided to ignore it. He texted back saying he thought we'd discuss things during our therapy session on Monday.

Long story short: we'd been in and out of both couples' and individual therapy over the years. This time, we had started attending as a family because of our son's academic struggles. But I suspect the therapist saw something else going on—because he suggested we meet without our son.

Still, I couldn't accept L.'s apathy or the blatant disrespect. I had a hard time controlling my anger when I got home. So, to make a point, I locked him out of the master bathroom that night. (To be fair, I did leave his glasses and contacts hanging on the doorknob.)

The next morning, he found me in the basement—my new hiding place—because by then I could no longer eat or sleep. I was waking up at 4:30 a.m. every day just to run or walk on the treadmill, trying to escape the gnawing pit in my stomach.

He opened with a half-hearted joke about me locking him out.

"Well, I was angry," I said. He got the point.

But then, as if that wasn't enough, he decided to twist the knife a little more by telling me all about his date the night before.

"Do you know the last name *[insert Gaelic-sounding last name here]*?" he asked.

I did. I recognized it immediately—it was the same last name as one of the Irish dancers from our daughter's dance school. That meant this woman's daughter and our daughter had likely been classmates.

"Well, this is going to be awkward," he said, with a smirk.

Then he launched into the details — how Bachelorette #3 was only 4'8" and had joked that people were probably staring at them as they walked into the restaurant because he's 6'4." I didn't find this amusing at all. Especially when he added that he'd had a good time on the date. (I know — you're wondering why I needed to know any of this. Trust me, it gets better. Just wait!)

After he finished his little highlight reel, he said he thought we should tell the kids about the divorce that day.

I agreed. He was the one who wanted out, so I let him take the lead.

That afternoon, we sat down with our son and daughter. Much to our surprise, they took the news fairly well. They said they weren't shocked—we'd been having trouble for a while, and apparently, they'd picked up on more than we realized.

Looking back, I'd describe them as *eerily* calm. Maybe they were just numb, like I was. Apathy can be a form of survival when there's been a slow starvation of love in the house.

L., however, was surprised by their reactions.

"They're so calm," he said, clearly thrown off.

"Well," I replied, "you were affected by your parents' fighting. Why wouldn't they be affected by ours?"

It also happened to be Father's Day, and I had no intention of celebrating this man in any way. I explained this to him. He said he understood and added that he would take the kids out to do something together. Just as I was getting ready to leave and run some errands, he remarked that he had something funny he wanted to show me. He hesitated for a moment because he thought I might be angry when I saw it — it was from Bachelorette #1 (let's call her "Stephanie," since that is her name). But I decided to let my curiosity get the better of me, so I looked at what was on his phone's screen, and this is what I saw:

This meme of a mom braiding her daughter's hair looks innocent enough—and it's meant to be light-heart-

ed. But for me, it was the conversation bubbles that landed like a mic drop. When the daughter asks her mom if she had wanted a son or daughter, the mom replies, "All I wanted to do was fuck."

Copyright attributed to the meme's creator, author unknown

I didn't know what to say. He thought it was hilarious!

I couldn't believe that my husband—who I had been with for almost 30 years—had such little regard for my feelings. I just looked at him and made some excuse about not being able to respond because of the anti-depressant I was taking. That wasn't even close to the truth. The reality? I wanted to rip his fucking throat out.

Now let's stop right here for a moment, because this interaction is extremely significant. Yes, my medication was dulling my senses, but there's more to this story than that. It has taken me a long time to fully understand what I was feeling in that moment—and what it revealed about the collapse of our relationship.

Here's how I would explain it now: L. had lied to me about wanting to have children, and that cartoon made it feel like he had told her the truth when he could never tell me. In that instant, I felt the wave of his resentment—resentment for having kids with me—crash over me. Apparently, he felt it was okay to joke about this with a stranger, but not to be honest with his wife. That's what it was in a nutshell.

At the time, our son was 18 and our daughter 15. He had been harboring resentment all those years—for a decision he made—to go ahead and have children.

Here's the backstory:

When we were planning our wedding, I wanted to honor both of our religions—his Lutheran, mine Catholic. We agreed to get married in his church, with a Catholic priest assisting his pastor. As part of the Catholic tradition, we had to complete a course for engaged couples called "Pre-Cana." It's a discussion group led by a married couple and a priest, where you talk through a variety of topics to ensure you're truly compatible. In theory, it should help reduce the number of divorces. You'd think.

But in our case, it was during Pre-Cana that my prospective husband, when asked if he wanted children, should have said "No." If he had, we wouldn't have ended up in this mess—because I would have ended the relationship then and there. And he knew that. Especially because his last girlfriend had broken up with him for that very reason. (I'm still friends with her to this day, and she told me how she made her decision to walk away.)

Instead, when I said I wanted four kids, he said he'd compromise at three—but that ideally, he would only want two. He added that he wanted us to wait five years before starting a family, so we could become more financially stable and settle into a house. At the time, that sounded reasonable to me, so I agreed. But five years later, a totally different conversation took place—and that's a story for later.

For now, I was in the thick of this debacle.

I left the house to run errands and stay as far away from him as possible. Doing routine things helped me feel normal in a very abnormal situation. I was like a zombie, walking around with all this pain I couldn't shed.

Toward the end of the day, as I reluctantly headed home, I got a call from our daughter.

"What should I make for dinner?" she asked.

"Where's your father?"

"He left," she said.

Puzzled, I called him.

"Hey, where are you?"

"Oh, I decided to run some errands. I'm going to visit Ted."

It sounded suspicious.

A) It was Father's Day, and he had said he was going to spend it with the kids—which clearly didn't happen.

And B) why would he choose to visit a friend who didn't have children over spending time with his own?

Still, I accepted his excuse. I think I was just too tired to care. I soon woke up, though.

When I got home, I decided to check in with the kids about the news of the divorce. They both said they were okay with it and that they would be fine. I felt oddly relieved by this—but it was short-lived. Our son went back to his room to play on his computer, while our daughter sat with me to watch TV.

A few minutes later, she flung her tablet on the couch and ran upstairs. I couldn't understand why she was acting that way—until I heard her shout, "Throw him out of the house!" I didn't know who she was referring to. I picked up the tablet and found a string of texts from one of her friends. He and his family had gone out to dinner for Father's Day, and who walked into the same restaurant but L. and Miss Stephanie! Not only did her friend inform her, but he sent along two pictures: one of L. strolling down the street, holding hands with a woman who wasn't her mother, and another of the two of them in an embrace. (To add insult to injury, he was even wearing a favorite t-shirt, which happened to have our wedding date on it.)

The medical term for an upset stomach is *functional dyspepsia*—a condition that causes discomfort or pain in the upper belly, near the ribs. Discomfort wouldn't hold a candle to how bad my insides felt. And are you familiar with the character "Anger" from *Inside Out?* Yeah, fire came out of my head too. I completely lost it. I picked up the phone and started screaming bloody blue murder at him. I told him to never come back to our home.

He laughed.

I was shaking with rage again. But after I hung up, something hit me: He needed to fix the situation—not me. So I called him back and said, "I apologize for my initial outburst, but your children are extremely upset. You should tell Stephanie—she's a mom, she'll understand—that you have to cut your 'date' short and come home to take care of your kids." He reluctantly agreed.

While waiting for him to return, I talked to the kids and told them they shouldn't calm down. He needed to see how upset they were. They agreed, and when our daughter had finished packing his bag, the three of us waited for him in the kitchen. Soon we heard him walking toward the door. I was caught between holding my breath and wanting to throw up.

He was defensive the moment he stepped inside, saying he was going to tell the kids about his affairs. But I stopped him before he could say another word. I don't know what came over me—I think I had finally had enough of all the bullshit. I held up my hand and said, "Hold that thought. I have something to say."

"What?" he asked.

Acting on impulse, I stepped back, moved my arm to the side, and bitch-slapped him across his right cheek.

IT. FELT. GOOD.

He stumbled backward, grabbing his face and crying out, "Oh my God! I can't believe you just hit me! Oh my God—did you guys see what your mother just did? I was going to talk to you, but now I'm not—I'm not staying!"

All 6 feet 4 inches of him was quivering because 5-foot-8 me slapped him. It wasn't funny at the time, but I can definitely laugh about it now.

Quickly realizing my mistake (sort of), I jumped into his car to stop him from getting away. Suddenly, the four of us—me, L., our son, and our daughter—were screaming and shouting at each other in our garage. It was chaos. He even called 911 but then told the operator he had dialed in error. The arguing continued until our daughter walked up to him, pointed, and yelled, "You're married! You shouldn't be doing that!"

To which he responded, "Don't get in my face!"

I'm honestly surprised the neighbors didn't come out to ask what the hell was going on. I thought for sure we were loud enough to rattle the whole block.

Eventually, by some grace of a Higher Power, our son got everyone to calm down. Ever the diplomat, he explained that this was a shock to him, to his sister, and to me, and that his father should take that into consideration. L. realized our son was right and started telling the kids that—since he and I had been having problems—he thought this was the best way to handle things.

He added, "I was very black and white about wanting the divorce, but I'm trying to be gray about the next 60–90 days because I don't know if this relationship will develop into anything... or I could fall back in love with your mom."

This is the part where you should be saying, like I did in my head, *WTF? Why would you say that to your kids? That's just cruel!* But I held that thought in the back of my mind because the next day we were going to see the therapist together. My head was spinning from all the confusion he was throwing my way.

As I said, I didn't want a divorce. I thought things could be turned around if we just worked together. But my dear friend Mary Ann—who was the first person I confided in—told me, "I don't know anyone who has worked as hard at their marriage as you have."

And she was right. I was finally realizing that, for all intents and purposes... I was alone in my marriage.

2

The Collective

Have you ever felt like you were in two places at once? Most people say you can't be, but I feel that way every single day. Whether it's geographic, political, social, or economic, I am always divided. Let me see if I can explain why. Just follow the bouncing ball that is my brain and bear with me as this next chapter is chock-full of fun-filled family facts! (In other words, it may seem boring compared to the last chapter, but I'm trying to make a point, and sometimes it takes me a while to get there. At least, that's what my brothers and sisters would tell me Every. Damn. Time. they interrupted me at the dinner table. But they're not writing this book, are they? Ha! No, they are not. So there.)

I want to use this section about the beginning of my life as a way to piece together how I ended up in the wrong romantic situation. While there's no exact formula for making a strong partnership, a foundation must be there. And I thought that because my parents had this, I would too. Double Jeopardy for What is Naïve? Please, Alex! I would like to say that my parents were perfect, but they had one fatal flaw as role models: they rarely fought, or at least, they only sometimes shared those moments. This lack of conflict resolution became my Achilles' heel, and I'm just now beginning to learn how to handle it properly.

My parents made a good team despite their differences. Doris Jane Seifried was born and raised in Buffalo, NY, and Thomas Patrick Berrian was a boy from the Bronx. They were only a year apart in age, but they were further apart in backgrounds. Mom's dad and his brother owned a butcher shop in Buffalo, so during the Depression, her family managed to stay afloat. She was one of six kids, four of whom survived to early adulthood. My dad was one of three boys. Both of his parents worked to put food on the table. At different times, his father was a cab driver and the manager of a liquor store. He also raised homing pigeons on the rooftop of whatever apartment building they lived in, since they moved around quite a bit. My paternal grandmother was a telephone operator for the Norcross Greeting Card Company, and when I was little, I would ask her to speak in her "telephone voice" because I thought she sounded so funny!

Mom moved to New York City after graduating from Nursing School. She was, in my humble opinion, a very glamorous single gal. She even made the pages of *The Buffalo Evening News* twice. The first time as the winner of a nursing scholarship, and the second time, she was profiled in a piece showcasing the life of a young nursing student. Once, when we were attending a family wedding back in Buffalo, I commented on how that city always seemed dreary and overcast. She replied, "Why do you think I left?" She was my hero for making her way in the world. And she embodied her profession with her nurturing and patient spirit, which made her a great mom as well.

Dad joined a seminary to be a priest but left because he, "liked girls too much." He graduated from both Fordham University and the City University of New York with an engineering degree and a teaching degree, respectively. He met my mom after completing his time with the Marines, for which he was drafted during the Korean War. They were fixed up on a blind date, and when I asked them what their first impressions of one another were, my mom said my dad was too quiet, and my dad said my mom talked too much, smoked too much, and had curlers in her hair when she arrived late (a habit I inherited from her—arriving late, not the curlers!). With assessments like that, can you imagine they went on to have six kids? They were married for 56 years before my mom passed away. Dad survived three more years after that with a broken heart.

I know they shared many of the same values, like having a close family and strong faith, and were both raised Catholic. And Dad was very strict about raising us in the Church as well. Every Sunday, from birth through adulthood, if we were home, we had to attend Mass. It even took him years before he allowed us to wear jeans! I resented his insistence on attending church. I'm sure it laid the groundwork for my independence later in life, but it was so hard as a kid to understand why we had to do what he wanted us to do—because church was BORING, first and foremost—and later it developed my hatred for hypocrisy, which I believe most organized religions are really good at.

It was especially baffling why my father was so attached to his religion when, years later, I learned his paternal side of the family had a long history with the Protestant Church. My great-great-great-grandfather was a Huguenot who fled France during the persecution by the Catholics, moved to Holland, and then his children left there for New Amsterdam. They landed in New York sometime in the early 1600s and settled in Queens and the Bronx. In fact, there's an island off the coast of Queens still in the family name, with a street also named after them. We understand the relative who acquired that land lost it in a bet, and it is now home to a wastewater treatment plant. I've been there, and it smells wonderful!

"Humble brag" is such a great expression to use here because when you tell people ancestral stories like owning an island, they're supposed to be impressed, but then when they hear how it's now a sewage plant, it brings that lofty point back down to earth. But that sums up my whole life—the yin and yang. Someone once told me I looked like I was born with a silver spoon in my mouth, but I wasn't. And this dichotomy permeates my entire being. My parents totally embodied that for me—my upper-middle-class mom and lower-middle-class dad. A dad whose ancestors actually came from lofty beginnings, then lost it all. He pulled himself out of hardship. What I didn't factor into the equation was the fact that my dad also came from a loving household, which gave him a very solid foundation to begin his life and carry it forward.

Our parents can be a big influence on us as we're growing up—good or bad. However, if you have siblings, they too play an important role in shaping you. As stated earlier, there were six of us Berrian kids—three boys, three girls. The real Brady Bunch. And we were THAT family— annoyingly (according to some of the neighborhood kids) goody-two-shoes kids with a squeaky-clean life. We had everything we needed: a roof over our heads, food on the table, heat and hot water on demand, and air conditioning. But I always thought we were poor. Or at least, my mom made me feel that way because when I would ask for something special or extra, she would say we couldn't afford it. I didn't know then that it was because if she bought something for me, she would also have to buy something more for the others. After all, she and my dad were children of the Great Depression, and they knew a thing or two about saving money. Fortunately, I adopted that lifestyle. My mom taught me to never pay full price for anything, and to this day, I try to live by that rule. Especially because I am a brand whore, and if I didn't shop at bargain stores or thrift, I would be living on the streets. Seriously, I am *that* bad.

Anyway, my parents started their marital life in Westchester County, NY—a beautiful area just outside of Manhattan with nice suburbs and, further north, countryside. They moved around quite a bit as they added more kids to the roster. First in New Rochelle, then Dobbs Ferry, Strathmore (or Scarsdale really), and then finally, my dad built my mom her dream home in Chappaqua. I'm naming these towns for a reason: if you are at all familiar with any of them, then they will probably evoke a sense of sophistication and class. And they were. They might still be today, but I haven't been in those areas for many years. The thing is that, up until we moved to Chappaqua, the residences were small. And eight people under one roof? It's going to be cramped. The house on Carolyn Lane had the space we needed—plus an acre and a half of property to boot. It wasn't finished when I started kindergarten, so I had to commute up the Bronx River Parkway. My poor mom had to get all six of us dressed, fed, and out the door before the crack of dawn for at least six months until we moved in. She must have been exhausted!

Unfortunately, my father lost his New York-based job only a year and a half later. He quickly landed a new one, despite being across the river in New Jersey. Unfortunately, we had to give up our idyllic life in the rural landscape. Don't get me wrong; I love New Jersey and am proud that it is my adopted home state. It's just very different for me because New York is in my bones and has a totally different energy than any other place I've ever lived. If you know, you know.

As the fifth of six, I didn't have any status. I wasn't the oldest, youngest, or middle child. And I was the only blonde daughter, so I really felt left out. My sisters and two of my brothers have beautiful red hair. For years, I hated my hair and blue eyes because I thought it was dull and ordinary! Secretly, I wanted to have the features of a girl who was a mix of French and Asian. I thought that would make me exotic and fascinating because I felt anything but. It didn't help that my sister, Jane, told me once that my yellow hair made me a "piss head." Yes, Jane, you said that! Don't worry—I'm sure I got you back years later. What are sisters for, after all?

Alas, Jane wasn't the only one to use me as a whipping post. My brothers Rich and George (the middle and younger brothers, respectively) were also relentless in their pursuit of "Let's see if we can make Nan cry today." They both loved to call me a dog and point out my many missteps—I have diary entries to prove it. Somehow, my oldest brother, Tom, stayed out of the fray. For the most part. I still remember a time when he and Rich told me that there were hornets bigger than humans living in a tree I would play under. I could have sworn I heard buzzing after they told me that.

Not surprisingly, I was also picked on outside of the home. Today it's called bullying. Along with being ostracized for being from the "wholesome" family and because I struggle with dysfunctions that make me misunderstand social cues and have trouble with self-control, my social life beyond my home's four walls was also miserable. There are many more issues that come with those difficulties, and I am only now beginning to understand how they impact me. Needless to say, back then, I had a hard time making friends. Moreover, my skin started to break out when I was only 10, so terms of endearment like "Freak," "You're weird," and "Zit face" were regular insults I heard.

There was one girl in particular who loathed me and made me acutely aware of her feelings as often as possible. Fortunately for me, she lived one block over, was in my Girl Scout troop, didn't seem to have an early problem with acne, and was popular. Of course, right? Her mom, dad, and brother were all pretty nice. I'm not sure why she didn't share their personality traits. Anyway, one year, my parents decided to rent a house on Long Island for the entire summer season because my paternal grandmother would summer there too. We had never done this before and would never do it again, as it proved to be too much for my mom to handle alone with six kids while my dad was three hours away still working. But one of them must have had the bright idea to invite these particular neighbors to visit us to make my mom feel better—and me worse. As soon as I was told "she" was coming, the dread set in. I had no escape!

Although I don't remember the exact details, the week turned out to be okay. We bonded. A little. I remember her telling me I wasn't that bad. Gee, thanks! At that point, I probably took her assessment as high praise. I still have picture evidence of her actually smiling as we sat on the beach one day. Well, as I re-examine it, maybe it's just a grimace because the sun was in her eyes. Regardless, any expectation I may have had that a friendship would develop was not to be. Just like in *The Breakfast Club*, she forgot about me and continued to walk on by at school. Oh well. Her loss. I always wondered why that movie hit home with me, and now I remember why.

Speaking of evidence, I also have my yearbooks from junior high. During eighth grade, a classmate told me his friend had a crush on me and wanted to ask me out. I felt it was a practical joke and didn't believe either of them. Sure enough, my so-called paramour inscribed my yearbook with, "I love every zit on your face." Nice.

The only time I felt special was when I was a little kid in Strathmore. We had neighbors who told my mom they thought I was cute and should be on television. So, they bought tickets for my mom and me to attend the taping of a television show called *Romper Room,* which was filmed in Manhattan.

Maybe you've heard of it or seen it. A precursor to *Sesame Street,* it was a live, national educational television program but was produced in local markets with different hostesses and a rotating group of children. The kids got to participate in various activities like crafts, sing-alongs, and reading time. More often than not, the same kids would be on the show for a whole week. It was marketed as an on-air kindergarten for kids who were 4 or 5 years old. It ran from 1953 to 1994. My episode probably aired in 1968 or 1969. I was thrilled because I was going to be on television and thought it would be exciting—maybe even the start of my stardom!

Anyway, back in the '60s, we would get dressed up for special occasions like this. You wore dresses, stockings, your best shoes, coats, hats, gloves, etc. Once we were ready, we took the train with my dad because he worked in New York City. He looked so handsome in his suit, overcoat, and hat. My mom was the eternal beauty in her smart dress, pretty coat, and hat. It's a shame we don't dress like that anymore. I love jeans, but that was the epitome of style.

I loved going into "the city." It was bright, colorful, and full of energy. And as crowded or grimy as New York City was in those days, there was never any element of danger. I'm sure I was nervous about getting lost if I let go of my mom's hand, but I don't think I was ever scared. I still feel so comfortable there after all these years.

Shortly after arriving at the studio, however, I found out I was not one of the kids chosen to be on the show during the week and was only going to be a part of the sitting circle for story time. I was pissed, to say the least. There went my chance to be somebody! I have to say that for a four-year-old, my anger was monumental for such a little person. I think the proper term is apoplectic. My joy went from 60 to 0 in the blink of an eye. I shut down. I stopped talking. My sadness became an inner rage, compounded by the fact that, as I sat down very sourly to hear the story, I realized I had already heard it!

So, I'm sitting there, fuming. Like a snow globe that has been shaken but whose swirling insides have nowhere to go. I'm not smiling, and I don't want to be there any longer. There are way too many tough emotions ruminating in my young body. Well, what do you think the younger me decides to do at the end of it all? Nothing! I just sat there. I wouldn't leave because I didn't know how to handle all of these things I was feeling. I was taught to be polite, so a public temper tantrum was not in the cards. Note to future self: suppressing emotions becomes a pattern in my life. Watch out for it.

The poor stage manager didn't know what to do and was trying to get me off the set. I wouldn't budge. My bottom was planted firmly on that ground. I think they might have decided to "send in the clowns" to help, because I remember looking up at Bozo the Clown (his show was on next) and I think I remember him saying, "Hi, little girl, it's time for you to go," or something along those lines. He didn't sway me. I'm not afraid of clowns, especially ones with squeaky voices. Finally, the desperate stage manager barked at my mom: "Lady, get your kid off the stage!" My mom must have been embarrassed, but she didn't show it, even after Bozo's sidekick, Mr. Green Jeans, gave us a look.

I don't remember how my mom handled my attitude, but I wouldn't be surprised if she wanted to quickly mitigate the circumstances in order to get back home to her other five offspring, who were being watched by my father's mother. When we arrived back at the house, my Nana asked me, "Why didn't you smile when the camera was on you?" and I told her the reasons I was mad. Nana didn't put up with bullshit and probably gave me an earful on being ungrateful. She definitely was good that way. I also realize now that this was a big lesson in expectations versus reality—something I still struggle with.

In the long run, I thought this was going to be my one and only brush with fame, and it didn't pan out very well. I was washed up at 4 years old! What I didn't realize then was that another opportunity would come along when I was in college, and I really, truly thought I was finally going to be an actress.

While attending Manhattan College (which is actually in the Bronx, by the way), I worked as a writing assistant for the public relations office. One day, my supervisor, Lydia, asked if I wanted to be in a commercial. Did I? Of course I did! She said she had been contacted by the nonprofit, *The Association for a Better New York,* because they wanted college students to appear in their new campaign to promote the city's higher educational institutions. My friend, Ralph, and I were chosen to represent our school. All we needed for our wardrobes were sweatshirts with our college name, jeans, and sneakers.

It was a fun day of meeting other students and learning the jingle, "New York City – it's a great college town!" I even added an extra step to the choreography, which the director loved (for some reason, I believe it may have been Joel Schumacher, of *Batman Forever* fame, and who was a NYC native). Alas, I was pulled from filming at the last minute because, as luck would have it, my white sweatshirt was not cooperating with the sun on that bright day. It kept blinding the cameraman. Foiled again! I was extremely disappointed, but not nearly as much as my 4-year-old self. I think I became resigned to the fact that I was not going to be who I had dreamed of being, despite all my years of singing, dancing, and acting since *Romper Room.* What I didn't take into consideration, though, was that it took more than those things combined—like going to professional auditions, for example. I don't think I ever did. Again, expectations versus reality!

But I digress. I know that over the years, as I struggled with my self-esteem, my mom tried to make me feel special. I believe she did with all of us kids because that's just the kind of mom she was. Yet, I never believed her reassurances. I felt that was part of her job, and her opinion didn't count. I was stuck for many years believing love for myself was going to come from an outside source that didn't even include my family.

I think this is because my dad wasn't always the perfect father. There never is, although I thought Mr. Rogers seemed pretty close. I clearly remember my dad as a giant. He was 6 feet tall, so I literally looked up to him when I was little. And he was playful! For example, he would bounce me on his knee, pretending to be an elevator. He would bounce me a bit, say "Elevator going up!" and bounce me a bit higher, then he'd say, "Elevator going down," and he would open his legs, and I'd drop between them. It was such fun! To this day, I love doing that to toddlers. It's a cute and sweet way to interact with them. And who can resist a toddler's laugh?

Unfortunately, my dad was absent for a big part of my life. The most significant time? Adolescence. He traveled a lot for his job and tried to make up for the time away from home by bringing us trinkets and souvenirs from his trips. Yet when it came to the important part—how to navigate the changes I was going through as I became a teenager—he was emotionally not there. You see, Dad was freaked out by my sisters and me as we each went through puberty. I say this because he ignored us. He became distant and short-tempered. He was no longer the fun-loving elevator guy. And I know it wasn't just me because I checked in with each of them and asked if they remembered him being that way when we each hit about 12. Diane said yes, most definitely she remembered him that way. Jane, however, said it didn't really bother her. She was more of a tomboy, after all, and has always been more easygoing than the rest of us. There isn't a lot that bothers her. At least, that's the way she seems! I really wish I had her level of confidence. Maybe someday.

I'm sure this is where we're all thinking I must have developed daddy issues from this. It certainly seems that way and could be a big reason I had persistent trouble with the opposite sex. It took me years of therapy to figure this out, and only after I was already married. This doesn't forgive L.'s actions, but it can explain my reactions to him in certain situations, like as I said earlier when he would be critical of me one minute and then want intimacy the next. In the early days of marriage, for example, I took this as a normal process of love. I brushed it off. I didn't understand that this was not how a true partnership should be and had a lot of growth to go through after our divorce before I found that missing puzzle piece and developed the greatest relationship of my life. During my marriage, however, as things progressed and the kids came along, the Spidey sense that I shouldn't be treated this way started to kick in. Yet I didn't know how to properly react to him and would usually say something like, "Oh, I know what you want," which he found denigrating. What I should have said, if I had had the balls, was, "You want sex, after criticizing my lack of cleaning skills, my cooking, the way I run the house in general, and my parenting of our two special needs children? Are you insane?" Instead, I timidly said what I said and then acquiesced because I was a good little wife and wanted to keep the peace.

It's funny what you can convince yourself of when you don't know any better. Like staying in a bad relationship because you mistakenly think you really love the other person. You even tell yourself things will work out if you try harder. Then they'll understand how much you love them! And love prevails, right? Right? Unfortunately, kids, this is the real story: you can't love anyone else until you learn to love yourself first. Otherwise, it just won't work. You and your partner need to be two whole or complete beings before you can add them to your Emergency Contacts list. Neither L. nor I had that capability in our case, so we were doomed from the start.

3

Mom Life Isn't All It's Cracked Up to Be

I always wanted to be a mom. That's because I had a great role model and was brought up in a loving family. Sure, I went through a phase where I considered becoming a lawyer after watching *LA Law* and admiring Susan Dey and her beautiful suits. Then I fell in love with journalism after watching *Lou Grant*, the successor to *The Mary Tyler Moore Show*, in which Mary's former boss runs a newspaper. It made me realize I had an appetite for curiosity. I love to talk to people. I love hearing their stories and exchanging thoughts and ideas. It just fills my soul to do this. And it's the only way to solve the world's problems, in my opinion.

But in my heart, I always just wanted to be a mom like mine. She was the best. Not perfect, but she loved perfectly. And despite Dad's temporary nonchalant behavior, my siblings and I knew we had each other no matter what. Over the years, that "what" has included the breakdown of marriages, careers, and health. All normal stuff in the post-War era.

Unfortunately, my journey from a young married woman to a mom would be filled with a lot of problems and anxieties that came from some unexpected places—starting with my husband-to-be. To begin with, when L. and I decided to marry, I insisted our wedding be at his Lutheran church, which was prettier, with a Catholic priest co-officiating. This was because being raised in different faiths can cause problems, and I didn't want to upset my still very strict parents by marrying outside their Church. I genuinely thought having two officiants would cover all of my bases. Double the holiness, I say!

There are many, many disappointing things about the Catholic Church that came to light as I was getting married, which contributed to my loss of faith—but I'll save all that "Sturm und Drang" for a podcast episode—either mine or yours. However, one good aspect of being married in a church run by celibates is that they require all couples to participate in the Pre-Cana meetings I mentioned earlier. In theory, these workshops are a way for couples to get to know each other on a more in-depth level. Over the course of a few weeks, the prospective groom and bride are given a series of questions to think about and answer. For example, how will you handle finances? Or, of course, you are asked if you will raise your child or children as Catholics. But don't worry if you answer "No," they won't kick you out. We were also asked how many kids we wanted. During that particular meeting, I said I wanted four. L. looked at me, paused, and said that was too many. He would compromise at three, but two was enough. He added that he wanted us to wait five years before we started our family, so we would be established in our careers and possibly have a house by then (we were living in a condo at the time).

I stupidly agreed because I was about to be his wife, and marriage was about compromise, right? Then, as we were celebrating our fifth anniversary at a beautiful restaurant, I told him I was ready to start our family and was going to stop taking my birth control pills. To say he surprised me with a negative reaction is an understatement. He went as ape-shit as he could in a public place. He accused me of ruining a perfectly romantic dinner by bringing up that subject in public. He went on to tell me he didn't want children after all and that it would just add stress to our relationship. Pretty prescient, I would say.

I should have left then. I told him his change of heart was a breach of contract. I could easily divorce him for lying to me all those years. I couldn't imagine my life without children. It wasn't just a wish—it was a deep, unshakable desire to recreate the home environment I had grown up in. I thought for sure my husband felt the same way, that he was just scared. After all, parenting is a heavy responsibility. Yet I couldn't forget how he beamed with love when he held my newborn niece. I figured he'd come around when he held his own child in his arms. I thought he'd change if I gave him the family and home environment he would be proud of. What I didn't know then was that it wasn't what he wanted. And I was too young, too inexperienced, to see this issue as a major red flag.

We fought about it for a few more years, and then, unexpectedly, I found myself pregnant. I miscarried between the 10th and 12th weeks. It was an awful experience, one I will never forget. I started to cramp before the bleeding came, and was sent to the hospital to wait for the D&C (dilation and curettage). The surgeon was so backed up, I had to wait for hours. During that time, I went into labor. Imagine never having given birth, only to have your hospital roommate, as you're screaming from an unknown pain, tell you, "You're actually giving birth." I was stunned. It was, without a doubt, one of the most horrific experiences of my life, and one I wouldn't wish on anyone. It wasn't just the physical pain—which was like a hot knife tearing through my insides, coupled with intense cramping that hit just when I thought it was over—but the loneliness. Despite being surrounded by people, I felt completely alone. I was really scared the pain would never end. The hospital staff didn't know what to do with me since I was waiting for surgery, and I begged them for anything to ease the pain as I sat on the cold hospital bathroom floor, throwing up into the toilet. Eventually, they did give me something, and by the time I went into surgery, I was numbed enough to forgive the medical community for failing—once again—when it came to caring for women.

L. wasn't there with me because neither of us realized how bad it would get. I told him he could go back to work, and in hindsight, I know he would have been there had he known. After I recovered from the surgery, he said he was willing to try for us to conceive again, but only because he recognized how important it was to me—not because he wanted it. At the time, I was just grateful he had agreed. It wasn't until after our divorce that I understood how much he regretted that decision. His decision.

Our son was born in 1999—a big, beautiful, healthy baby. L. was thrilled we had a boy, and he led me to believe this was the start of our loving family.

That family unity didn't last long, though, when I told him I wanted to stay home with our son. By then, I had been working as a freelance writer for a marketing company. They were kind enough to give me a year-long assignment so I could work remotely, which was unusual for that time. I had been fortunate to work for a woman who had children herself and she understood how important it was for me to try to balance my job and motherhood.

But my inability to organize, plan, and prioritize correctly made it difficult to juggle the demands of a new baby and the assignment. And don't even get me started on trying to keep a clean home—another constant battle in our marriage. My ex-husband had been raised by a mom who kept her home spotless—like a German Felix Unger on steroids. Seriously, the woman vacuumed her walls! I could never compete with those mad skills, but L. sure expected me to.

Over the next two years, I had two more miscarriages. The second one was especially heartbreaking. Not only did I lose hope that our son would ever have a sibling, but the fetus never developed. The doctor explained that it had likely been reabsorbed by my body in a process called fetal resorption. According to Google's AI, "This occurs when one or more fetuses disintegrate and are assimilated into the uterus after organogenesis." I was heartbroken—not just for myself, but for the potential baby who never had a chance. My doctor kindly explained that it was probably for the best, as the baby would have likely had severe developmental disabilities and wouldn't have survived. It was a bitter pill to swallow.

My third miscarriage was almost the last straw. I had all the typical pregnancy signs—a missed period, a positive test, and surging hormones. We even heard the heartbeat. Unfortunately, once again, it wasn't meant to be, and I miscarried. The Ob/Gyn staff left me alone in the exam room so I could cry my heart out. Honestly, I can't remember if L. was with me when I got the news. It didn't really matter, though, since he had already made it clear that this was my journey to face.

After miscarriage #2, my doctor suspected I might be perimenopausal. I was 36 at the time and couldn't quite wrap my head around it. He said it was rare, but my eggs could be aging, and in the midst of this devastating situation, I actually laughed when he mentioned eggs—it made me feel like a chicken! Sure enough, at his suggestion, we checked my Follicle Stimulating Hormone (FSH) levels after miscarriage #3. And there it was, staring me in the face: my body was betraying me. I felt like a failure.

I took a nosedive into depression and I became comfortable there. I should have been grateful for my son, but I couldn't let go of the idea of having another child. I was almost obsessive about it, believing that having siblings meant my son would never be alone. I even started asking friends with one child if they wanted more, hoping they'd wave a magic wand over me and tell me it was okay for my son to be an only child. As it turned out, some of them had no choice—they had children later in life and were incredibly thankful just to have been able to conceive at all. Still, I was in my mid-30s, and I couldn't accept that my fate might be the same.

My doctor suggested we consult with specialists to see if there was any way to conceive again. I wavered between hope and desperation. I devoured research on why women my age experienced these challenges and sought advice from every possible source in search of answers. L. was patient and seemed to understand how important this was to me. We even discussed the possibility of adopting. Then again, when an adoption agency hosted a seminar about the process, I can't recall whether he attended with me or not. Isn't that odd?

He was, however, there when we went to the fertility clinic. In fact, when we learned our chances of conceiving again were very low, and the cost of in-vitro fertilization was sky-high, he suggested we go through a certain point in the process and then decide whether to continue. As he pointed out, with adoption, you're guaranteed a child, but with in-vitro, you're not. I understood his logic and agreed. So, we started with genetic testing, blood work, and a little-known test called the hysterosalpingogram. The most surprising result for me was that I have a mutated MTHFR gene—what my cousin Cathy affectionately calls the "Mother Fucker" gene (because she has it, too). While a mutated gene doesn't always cause problems, alterations can lead to serious health issues such as cardiovascular disease, strokes, and birth defects. Unfortunately, Cathy had a stroke and lost a baby. Knowing this, I didn't take the information lightly, and was told I would be closely monitored if I ever became pregnant again.

Now, the hysterosalpingogram (HSG) was a different story. The fertility clinic said it was a routine procedure to check for scar tissue in the uterus, as well as blockages in the fallopian tubes and ovaries. Friends of friends had undergone the test before me and said it was a good step to take. Research also showed that some women can conceive after it has been performed. The theory is that even if no blockages are detected, the procedure helps clean out your system, preparing your body to accept an egg. I asked L. if it was okay to try for another baby afterward, and he told me it was my decision since it was my body. I was ready to give it a go.

My mom came with me the day of the procedure. I don't remember too many details since it took place over 20 years ago, but I do remember the pain! The HSG is an X-ray in which they shoot dye up your lady bits (or cooter, glory hole, or whatever you call her), and then the doctor examines the images. I never knew a simple colored liquid could cause so much discomfort and sharp pain. Regardless, I was told my parts were clean as a whistle and was given permission to go ahead and try to get that baby in the oven.

And we did! The way I found out was pretty surreal, too. I missed my period and took at least two home pregnancy tests, both of which came back negative. I didn't feel the same as when I found out I was pregnant with our son. I wasn't overly tired, I didn't have breast tenderness, and my stomach didn't seem bloated. I was convinced something was wrong again, so I made an appointment with the fertility clinic for an exam. I explained my situation to the nurse assigned to me, and she suggested an internal ultrasound to check for a missed blockage. Well, lo and behold, the attending physician and the two nurses assisting her were delighted to inform me the scan showed I was expecting another baby! I couldn't believe it. I asked her to repeat what she said. They were all smiling. I was in total shock, and instead of elation, dread set in. Was I going to lose this one too? I called L. to share the news, and he seemed genuinely happy. I had to tell my parents, too, because they were cheering me on. They knew how important motherhood was to me, and they wanted me to have the family I wanted.

Our daughter arrived nine months later, but not without complications along the way. Early on, I started to bleed. While we were visiting friends in the Adirondacks, L. and I took our son on a tour of Fort Ticonderoga. I discovered the spotting when I went to use the bathroom and started to panic. My heart began to race, and I impulsively purchased a teddy bear in the gift shop so I could cling to it as we wandered the grounds. I didn't experience any cramping, but I just felt like something was wrong or was going to be.

Following my third miscarriage and during my depression, I did some extensive research on what causes infertility. Over the years, I've found research to be a very good coping skill for me. I enjoy learning new things and sharing that knowledge with others, especially when it comes to problem-solving. Anyway, I read an article in a women's magazine about a doctor who was a developmental pathologist. What this means is she's a research scientist who examines tissue samples for deformities. At the time, she was running a private practice for women who had multiple miscarriages and would consult with them and their doctors after examining tissue samples from their incomplete pregnancies. What the doctor concluded was that the arteries in my uterus appeared to be extremely narrow, which may have caused inflammation and hypertension with my past pregnancies. She suggested I be monitored with a Doppler ultrasound during my next pregnancy to watch for any blood flow issues. When the bleeding started, she was the first person I called to ask what to do. Her calm demeanor helped, but I was still so afraid of losing another baby. L. suggested we head home, and I gratefully agreed. I clung to the gift shop bear the whole way back. I still have it today.

I jokingly say my daughter is my last good egg, and she truly is. She is my heart and soul, and I was thrilled to have a little girl. Don't get me wrong, I loved having a boy, too, because I thought that was what L. wanted, and because our son was a delight. He ate and slept like a champ and has always had a great sense of humor. He is also super smart, although he doesn't believe that about himself. Unfortunately, his special needs didn't become apparent to us until he reached high school, which made his educational journey a struggle. I applaud him for continuing to move forward every day, including graduating college. That's all we can ask of ourselves.

As a little girl, I loved playing "family" with my dolls as I dreamed of my rosy future. I also had a good relationship with my mom, which I wanted to continue into the next generation. However, my first impression of my daughter was not great; she didn't seem to have eyebrows, making her look like an alien. Sorry, honey! Plus, she must have had bad reflux because projectile vomiting was common for her. She cried a lot from the discomfort, so L. suggested we have her sleep in her car seat at the bottom of our bed in order to be upright and avoid continual heartburn throughout the night. The poor kid had it rough from day one. Adding to that, throughout her gestation, I was so anxious about losing her that I truly believe I passed on that mental health issue through the womb.

Once, a therapist asked me if being a mom was fulfilling for me. It definitely was not. I think that was for two reasons. The first was that L. made it very difficult. For example, when our son was a baby, I loved playing with him. One day, L. came home from a client appointment, saw me on the family room floor playing a game with our son, and said, "What are you doing that for? You shouldn't be playing with him. You should be taking care of the house." Having a clean home was extremely important to him. Unfortunately, I was not capable of meeting his expectations. Clutter on the kitchen and dining room tables was a common occurrence that I still struggle with.

The second reason a happy motherhood escaped me was because I had been a full-fledged, Melanie Griffith-like *Working Girl* before I was married and had kids. I even moved out of my parents' home a year after graduating college. I shared apartments in Hoboken and Montclair, New Jersey, and had my own place in Riverdale, New York, a few blocks from my alma mater. I learned to be independent, and I relished it. As one of six kids, it was important to me to have my own life and identity. Being from a big family is great, but sometimes you need to break away.

I started working at the age of 16 when my mother told me to. She said that she and my dad would continue to provide my needs (food, clothing, and shelter), but I had to start paying for my wants (entertainment, designer jeans, jewelry). My first job was as a Page in our local library, which I really enjoyed, but I believe I was eventually fired for talking too much. No one who knows me will be surprised by this!

By the time I met my husband, I was paying my own bills and managing my single life better than he was, since he didn't leave home until we bought our condo before the wedding. Yes, his mother cooked for him and did his laundry until he moved into our home at the age of 26. Shoulda seen that one coming.

And although I envisioned a glamorous writing career, I never accomplished that goal. I earned a degree in Communications from Manhattan College (now Manhattan University) and landed jobs in publishing as an editor. I also worked in public relations, where most of the writing was press releases and newsletters—not the kind of writing I had dreamed of doing. I should have stuck with journalism, but I'll tell you why I didn't. I blame an award-winning journalist with News 12 New Jersey, Walt Kane. We attended college together, but he's a few years older than me. From what I remember, he knew he wanted to be a journalist from an early age, although he was unsure of that career choice when he entered college. But the fates pushed him in the right direction, and as he was about to graduate, he landed a job. Our Journalism teacher, Sr. Patricia, announced his accomplishment to the class. She was so proud of him, and we were all excited as well. The only problem, as I saw it, was that he had to start his career in the Midwest—Iowa, I believe—and would be making very little money. I didn't want to end up that way. I wanted to work in the Big Apple, dammit, and was afraid I couldn't afford to move out of my parents' home if I made a small salary. That's why I switched my concentration from journalism to public relations; I knew I would make more money that way. Ultimately, though, just like Julia Roberts said in *Pretty Woman*—Big mistake! Huge!

Now, why did I bother pursuing a career in anything when all I wanted was to be a mom? Good question. The fact is, I wanted to live an independent life before settling into the motherhood role. The problem is, in order to do that, you have to make money. And independence, to me, meant renting an apartment, buying your own food, paying for utilities, or being able to cover your expenses no matter what. These are all things that need to be paid for, and in the NY-metropolitan area, those things can be really expensive. Unfortunately, because I ended up pursuing the almighty dollar more often than not while building my resume, I jumped from job to job and never proved myself anywhere.

Yet, I identified as a working woman. Having my own bank account and living outside of my parents' home—whether on my own or with roommates—was a part of my persona. I was used to the 9-to-5. I was used to complaining about my bosses (not you, Fred!), my coworkers, the company I worked for, the work I was doing, etc. It was routine, and I relish routines. There was a sense of accomplishment in managing my own life. Looking back, I'm really proud of myself for being able to do that, especially when I lost my job once and was still able to find a way to pay my rent that didn't involve wearing fishnet stockings. My desire to be on my own kept me in the workforce.

L. assumed I would always be a working woman and was counting on life to continue that way after we had kids. I truly thought I would go back to work as well. But something changed. I was going through menopause and some postpartum depression when I started to become agitated about leaving our son with anyone else. I remember lying in bed, and as soon as I started to picture my infant with anyone else, a panic attack would start. For me, this meant my heart would freeze and then race at fast intervals. It was unnerving, to say the least. When I gathered the courage to tell L. I wanted to be a stay-at-home mom, he was less than enthusiastic and told me that if that was what I wanted, then in addition to running the household, the children would be my sole responsibility. I didn't argue because I felt I could do it.

Frankly, deciding to stop working was a very, very difficult decision. I not only lost my independence, I lost my autonomy. I lost my capability to take care of myself financially, which, in turn, led to feeling like a prisoner. I thought that by having children, I was gaining a family. Instead, I was losing everything I had worked for. Oddly, however, I gained it all back through this divorce. I just didn't know it at the time, when my world was crashing all around me.

4

Hello Darkness, My Old Friend

Depression has been a familiar part of my life. My brother had a severe battle with it as a young adult, and I attempted suicide when I was 16. It's actually a funny story.

I struggled a lot in school, both academically and socially—just like my own kids did. I was never diagnosed with a learning disability like my daughter was, nor with Asperger's like my son, but I was in and out of remedial classes for English, Math, and Speech. I even had to go to the trailers in high school, since that was the only place they could fit us "extra specials." That part especially sucked because my remedial Math class took place during everyone else's Music History lessons. And I love, love, love music. It makes my heart happy!

Once, my remedial Math teacher was absent, and I had the pleasure (I say, sarcastically) of taking part in just one of those precious Music classes. I remember the teacher asking all sorts of questions about different music styles, instruments, etc., and as she was doing so, many of the answers were firing off in my head. I couldn't stand it, so I decided to answer under my breath, since I wasn't an official member of her roster. For example, when she asked, "Which style of music originated in the United States?" I quietly answered, "Jazz." As it turns out, one of the football jocks overheard me and started repeating what I said. Not surprisingly, he got the credit—and I got angry.

And not just the temporary kind of anger—the clenched fists and tight jaws that eventually go away. No, it was the festering, snow-globe kind that led to the beginning of my pure hatred for the American educational system.

I also mentioned earlier how I was blessed around age 10 with a face full of persistent acne that stuck around throughout high school. Some girls had the knack for covering theirs with heavy makeup, but I wasn't allowed to do that. My mom didn't even want me wearing mascara or black clothing because it was "too mature for your age." I had no way of hiding my hideousness. Is it any wonder I felt like shit?

It all came to a head one night. Exhausted, exasperated, and probably embarrassed by the fact that I could barely understand what I was learning in school—coupled with my social anxiety and the fear that I would never, ever find someone to love me—I decided to take my own life. Sort of.

My family had all gone to bed. I couldn't sleep. I walked into the kids' shared bathroom, opened the medicine cabinet, and found a bottle of pills. I took out a handful and stared at them in my hand. I looked at myself in the mirror. Was I ready to do this? How would it feel? Did I really want to die?

I could hear my mom snoring down the hall. Otherwise, it was quiet—except for the noise of the turmoil inside me. Suddenly, something made me stop, and I threw the pills into the sink and washed them away.

I don't know why, but I woke up my parents to let them know what I had been trying to do. I'm sure it was part attention and part reassurance. Either way, I was crying my eyes out, snot flowing freely. The great parents that they were, they comforted me and suggested we talk more the next day.

So, where's the funny part in all of this?

Well, the next morning I decided to look at what those pills were exactly. Turns out one of my siblings had pink eye, and the pills had been prescribed to alleviate it. Even if I had swallowed them, I doubt anything would've happened.

But that feeling—that desperate feeling of wanting to end it all—still visits me every once in a while, even to this day. Thankfully, it occurs a lot less since the divorce.

Yet I'm a fighter. Or maybe it's just stubbornness. Could even be persistence. A little of all three? Regardless, I started therapy when I was 18, as a freshman in college. Here's another funny story: I decided I was ready to begin my mental health journey then because—wait for it—I didn't understand boys! Or sex! After all, I was a virgin, and I was one confused girl. That lack of social awareness came back to haunt me as the divorce unfolded, but at the time, it was the main reason I walked into Dr. Gilbart's office on the Manhattan College campus. When I realized he was my friend's father, and that it was going to be incredibly awkward to discuss my thoughts and feelings about intercourse with middle-aged him, he graciously suggested I switch to his female colleague. She was nice, but she couldn't help me much—mostly because I didn't understand how to help myself.

Subsequently, drinking in college became my escape plan. It was a fun pastime for forgetting my pain. There are a few of you reading this who might remember those special nights when I blacked out, and you were kind enough to recount my antics later—like the time I tried to bite a balloon tied to someone's wrist, or when I was so plastered I couldn't remember how to get back to my dorm room and you graciously walked me there. This "good behavior" earned me the title of *Class Flirt*, because my drunken self was that obnoxious party girl who became emboldened with every drink. I guess you could say I'm not one to hold on to shame, which is why I'm open to talking about it.

By some sort of miracle—and a little bit of medical—I contracted mononucleosis my senior year and was told by the doctor to stop drinking because it would damage my liver. I did—for exactly the time frame he suggested. When the weeks passed, I resumed drinking and can still remember the severe pain that followed. I haven't been able to, nor have I wanted to, recreate those drunken days or nights since. But I still enjoy alcohol. I just know my limits now.

Although my sobriety continued after college, my depression did too. It's gotta be in the genes, because I passed it on to my children. Each has had their own suicidal experiences, which is heartbreaking. My only hope is that it has given them a strength they might not otherwise have had.

Over the years, I've collected therapists like trading cards and racked up countless counseling sessions. It wasn't until around the nineteenth year of marriage, however, that I added an antidepressant to my therapy. It was prompted by my mom dying. She had been diagnosed with osteoporosis, and her body was slowly decaying. She eventually succumbed to the effects of it. Anyone who says you can't die from this disease doesn't know what they're talking about—and my current endocrinologist agrees. You can die from osteoporosis, because your body collapses in on itself. In my mother's case, like so many others, it became impossible for her to breathe properly. She would expel carbon dioxide but then breathe it right back in, since her face was that close to her chest. Her lungs weren't clearing. She had a mass inside that was strictly just liquid she couldn't get rid of. It was painful for her—and painful for us to watch her go through it. She passed away on August 19, 2011, at 83 years old. That was a long life, but I could still use her here today. My whole family feels the same way.

Amid my divorce, I had the bright idea to come off my antidepressants. They made me feel stuck, like I was walking through quicksand. And I knew I would eventually need to take control of my situation, instead of letting things happen to me, as I had been doing. For example, I had been in charge of my finances before marriage, but without a salary now, I had nothing to manage. After my dad passed away in 2014 (three years after Mom, and unofficially from a broken heart), I inherited some money—and it would have been enough for me to leave my husband and start a new life… *if* I had had a job. As luck would have it, L. convinced me to roll that money into our joint investment account, insisting it would be used for our retirement. Knowing it would be difficult to withdraw that amount without raising suspicion, I remained frozen in my bad situation. I also felt I couldn't get a job for a few reasons.

I had made an agreement with L. to go back to work when the kids were old enough to attend school, and I thought that would happen easily. But as they were growing up, my career was being phased out. Most of my job experience was in print publishing—working as a writer, editor, and proofreader. One of my favorite roles was as the copy editor for a weekly travel newspaper. Taking our reporters' words and honing them into coherence was fun. Our top journalist even complimented me on being able to turn his "gibberish into something that makes sense." The rush of completing everything before the print deadline was exhilarating, too.

Then came the digital age—and it made my work obsolete. Everywhere I turned, companies were looking for people with online experience. I was told over and over again that my background in print didn't translate to digital, especially once the new language—Search Engine Optimization (SEO)—became a thing. On top of that, I couldn't convince L. to spend the money on additional classes since I already had a bachelor's degree. I think it was mostly because he could teach himself things and didn't understand why I couldn't teach myself. Our kids' learning disabilities should have been a clue for both of us; those genes had to come from somewhere.

Pivoting to a different career was a consideration, but I couldn't figure out what I wanted to be when I grew up. I applied for retail positions—my longest-running gig from high school through college—and interviewed in other industries, but nothing came through. It was discouraging and humiliating to realize that the years I'd spent building a career didn't amount to anything. Eventually, I did a bit of freelance writing, but that didn't help pay the bills. So, my only real job experience became entertaining the diaper crowd.

Losing your identity and trying to build a new one is not easy. On top of that, motherhood wasn't turning out the way I'd hoped. Even though I was raising two human beings, I didn't feel like I had a purpose. And while the antidepressants helped me maintain my sanity, I felt like now I needed to pull up my Big Girl panties and try to manage things naturally instead of artificially.

That's when I discussed my plan to drop the medication with my family doctor. After he and his Nurse Practitioner expressed concerns about my timing, they told me to cut the dose in half. I learned the hard way that this was not the best method. Within a short amount of time, I was a wreck—a train going off the tracks. I felt like I was on speed. (Not that I've ever taken it—it's just what I imagined it to be like.) One minute my heart was fine, and the next it was racing. My mind wouldn't stop jumping from thought to thought, and when I sat down, my legs wouldn't stop tapping. I thought I was either going to die from the stress or kill myself because of it.

One day I even asked my brother, Rich, to come over and just sit with me because I didn't think I'd make it through the rest of the day. I was scared. Eventually, I thought I was returning to some semblance of normal, but after Rich went home, I spiraled again and knew I had to take action. I couldn't take it anymore. I told my kids they needed to take me to the hospital. Can you imagine having your 15- and 18-year-old children care for you because you think you're going to kill yourself from stress? My mental state was stretched like a rubber band.

But even in the midst of chaos, I kept my mom-sense and tried to turn it into a teachable moment. As my son and daughter waited with me in the ER (and why did they change it to ED? Those initials just remind me of penile dysfunction), I told them to never be embarrassed to ask for help. They both said they understood. It was a sweet moment—they sat with me on the gurney, hugged me, and did their best to lift my spirits. I don't know if they'll ever know how much that meant to me. They're such good people.

The ER staff was kind. They gave me some Xanax and told me to use it as needed. It worked for a few hours, but by the next morning, I was off to the races again. This time, my dear friend, Jenny, offered to take me to the hospital. And this time, I knew what to do: I was ready to get myself admitted to the psych ward.

The night before, I had dodged the question about whether I was suicidal. Not today. Today was it. I knew I needed to be locked up. I knew it was the only way to get to the bottom of things—before I ended up at the bottom of water. I took a deep breath, and when they asked if I was planning to kill myself, I said yes.

After all, I did have a plan.

I will always have that plan.

And now? It doesn't involve pills for pink eye.

Soon enough, I was heading up to the second floor. I don't know if every hospital's psych ward is at the same height—just high enough that if you jump out a window you'd only injure yourself—but since I've only been in this one, I can only give you insight into this particular establishment. IT WAS GREAT! Sure, the beds were wooden platforms with very thin foam mattresses, but hey, they won't kill you!

Aside from that, imagine a calm environment with quiet background noise and a caring staff. It was like a spa! The food was surprisingly good, we played games, had group discussions, and even welcomed guest speakers (someone get "TED" in there—what a captive audience!). It was peaceful. For the first time in weeks, I was able to sleep and rest. Honestly, I almost didn't want to leave.

And truthfully, I couldn't. As soon as you arrive, you're locked in. That might be scary for some, but for me, it was a relief. I knew I was in a safe place, and I was confident I would get the help I needed—if I chose to accept it.

My ex and the kids even came to visit one day. They all remarked on how happy and good I seemed. L. even said I looked like my old self. I was glad to hear it—and I believed him. Foolishly, I started to think maybe we could have a peaceful transition out of our marriage. Boy, was I wrong about that. But in that moment, I enjoyed the kindness of my family—especially from the one who had hurt me the most.

Before my first stay ended, the hospital staff switched me to a new antidepressant. It's similar to the one I had been on and the psychiatrist thought it might be a better fit since some family members had success with it. Well, maybe it worked for them, but for me? Not so much.

Shortly after starting it, I experienced the same awful symptoms again—like I'd become a regular customer of Walter White's.

Back to the Loony Bin I went!

Now, let me take a moment to remind you, dear reader, that this story is based on my personal experience. If you're offended by my un-politically correct language—too bad. I am one of those people who can find humor in bad situations. And I had a very good experience in the psychiatric unit of my then-local hospital. I know not everyone does, and I'm truly sorry for those who haven't. But I want to shine a light on the fact that a very serious situation doesn't have to be all doom and gloom.

In fact, the nurses were incredible. They made it as pleasant as possible—and they don't get enough credit for what they do. Yes, I'm biased—my mom was a nurse—but it takes something extra to work in a place where you're probably rarely thanked and regularly (literally and figuratively) defecated on.

Fortunately, none of that happened while I was there. It was even fun at times. There were usually 8–10 patients in the unit, and since it was August, we all looked forward to being let out into the courtyard on sunny days.

The only time I felt uneasy was during my second stay. A patient who had just been released from prison joined us. He was clearly an addict and pretty funny at first, but when he joked about wanting to shoot people walking past our windows, I got a little leery.

Round 2 in the ward also marked the beginning of the end—not just of my marriage, but of my patience with L. and his behavior.

After my first stay, L. had said, "If you need anything, let me know." Noble, right? So, I took him up on the offer and asked him to drive me back to the hospital. He picked me up and drove me to the medical center—while regaling me with stories of his dating adventures with Miss Stephanie.

Apparently, she had told him he needed more experience dating other women, then flipped out when he actually took her advice and reactivated his dating profile. Mon dieu! After consulting two of his friends, L. decided to break up with her.

Should I say I was relieved for him? Or that I didn't give a shit?

I asked him to stop sharing those stories—it hurt my feelings—and he apologized. But why did I have to ask in the first place?

As we sat in the waiting room, everything started to crash around me. I couldn't believe the person sitting across from me was the same man I had devoted most of my adult life to. I felt hollow and sick, but made one feeble attempt at asking him if we should reconcile.

He looked at me and said no—he had moved on.

That was actually the kindest thing he could have done for me. The door was shut and locked.

He walked with me into the ER to make sure I was taken care of. When you're on Suicide Watch, they assign an aide to monitor you. Once mine arrived, I told L. he could go. And then I made some snide remark about how happy I was that we were parting ways.

It wasn't the last time I'd see him that year, but it was the last time I'd ever consider letting him back into my heart.

I finally admitted to myself: he was never, ever going to be the man I wanted—or needed—and there was nothing I could do about it.

And he's continued to prove that ever since.

As I've said before, I live my life out loud and believe in being honest and raw about my experiences. That day catapulted me even further in that direction. For example, the first aide had to leave when her shift ended. Lo and behold, a familiar figure replaced her. The curtain in my room opened, and in walked one of my neighbors! I was delighted to see her. Our sons used to have playdates together, and she always struck me as a strong woman. I couldn't help but exclaim, "Hey Sue, what are you doing here?"

When she explained she was working, I blurted out, "Well, I'm in because I'm on Suicide Watch." She kind of chuckled and remarked that was exactly why she was there—she was my next aide. Let me tell you, it was a comfort to spend the next few hours with her. She was kind and forthcoming about her own struggles. She totally helped me relax and decompress. She was even there when the Nurse Practitioner came in with the diagnosis of Bipolar Disorder 2 (BP2).

I was confused, since no one in my family had ever been diagnosed with anything more than Attention Deficit Hyperactivity Disorder (ADHD) or depression. I asked why BP2 was a consideration and was told it was because the other NP and the staff psychiatrist thought my reactions suggested I was being triggered by the antidepressants—and that since BP2 is milder than BP1, maybe I had been experiencing symptoms without realizing it. She suggested I try a medication called Seroquel, and I agreed.

I was already familiar with the medication because a former sister-in-law took it. I knew it was an antipsychotic originally developed to help veterans cope with the severe effects of war and PTSD. I was concerned it might be strong, but I was willing to give it a try. And I'm really glad I did. Within a short period, I felt calm. Like buttah.

The NP was happy it was helping and said her team wanted to add Lithium (the drug, not the battery acid, although they are from the same ingredient) to my mental health "diet" as well. At that point, I was like, "Bring it on!" I wanted to be better, and I wanted it to happen NOW. But I was also grappling with the idea that I'd been harboring a condition I hadn't realized I had—and I was confused about how I ended up that way.

Most people who know me know that once I got out of the hospital, my next step was to do some research about what bipolar disorder was. I LOVE research. However, it can take you down a rabbit hole if you're not careful, and sometimes, I wallow in those holes. But I think it's really important to find the "Whys" before you can get to the "What-to-dos." And I needed answers, especially because one day I was just an averagely depressed, soon-to-be-divorced woman—and the next, I was a woman with a bipolar disorder. It felt strange being there.

Now, for those curious minds who like to learn like I do: there are two types of bipolar disorder, formerly known as manic depression. Bipolar 1 is the version most often misrepresented in the entertainment industry—the classic character who's outlandish one minute and weeping the next. The only good representation I've ever seen is Anne Hathaway's portrayal in *Modern Love* on Prime. That piece clearly showed what bipolar 1 mania is: the feeling of being high without taking any substances. Her character, Lexi, is impulsive and fun. She also appears quite intelligent one minute and then crashes into a deep depression at the slightest trigger.

Although both bipolar 1 and 2 involve mood swings, the mania in bipolar 2 can be so mild it's mistaken for something else, like general cheerfulness. Meanwhile, the depression often lasts longer than in bipolar 1. This can lead to devastating consequences like job loss, broken relationships, or financial ruin.

The hospital's psychiatric staff couldn't make a diagnosis based solely on my behavior, so they asked a few key questions. The one I remember most went something like: "Have you ever had a time in your life when you felt so intent on completing a task that you couldn't focus on anything else?"

My mind immediately went to a ridiculous incident when I decided to give away my kids' McDonald's Happy Meal toys because they weren't playing with them anymore. I spread them out on the family room floor, started sorting them while watching TV, and pieced them together (some came with accessories). L. was annoyed and said I was wasting time. He suggested I just toss them in a bag and be done with it, since I was donating them anyway. I just couldn't. My anxiety wouldn't let me. I *had* to present them to the local thrift shop in their original forms—even if they were only going to sell for a dollar!

When I was pregnant with our son, I did something similar—writing to companies and asking them to remove my name and address from unwanted catalogs. I was persistent because the sheer volume of mail was giving me anxiety. My partner objected to this task too, telling me I should be doing something else with my time.

Those two incidents were the basis for my diagnosis, according to the questions I was asked. Did I waste time? Sure. But did I sleep with multiple partners, abuse substances, or plunge us into financial ruin with impulsive shopping or gambling? Nope. Still, my positive answer to that one simple question led the mental health professionals—and me—to believe I was now in the bipolar disorder league. Mild or not.

One thing I knew for sure, though, was this: I wasn't going back to the same old me. My diagnosis was new, and now, my life was too.

I started to sleep again—soundly this time—and slowly began to regain both my physical and mental strength. It took a while to recognize I was getting better, but it happened. For example, L. stopped by the house on the Fourth of July, just before my hospitalizations. Our daughter had a few friends over to swim, and I had asked their parents to stay and hang out with me. L. had texted, asking if he could come over to talk. I said yes, expecting he'd show up after my guests had left.

But he came earlier and sat in the family room while I entertained my guests on the porch. When I told my friends he was waiting to talk, they agreed it was odd.

Turns out, he wanted to process his feelings about the demise of our marriage—and tell me how my medication was affecting my libido. He had learned this from Stephanie and apparently felt it necessary to share the information with me. That was a "no shit, Sherlock" moment, because—as the Research Nerd I am—I had already found that out on my own. I refrained from being rude and simply said, "Yeah, I know."

As he talked, I kept repeating in my head, *Please don't ask if you can move back in. Please don't ask if you can move back in.* Over and over.

After I got out of the hospital, I replayed that visit in my head and realized something: I was ready to move on, too. That was my first step in knowing—I was going to be okay.

5

My Rumspringa

After a hospital clears you from the psych unit, you're usually assigned some form of group or individual therapy—or both. My hospital assigned me to group therapy for a set period of time, and I also had a caseworker.

The best part about "Group," as it's affectionately called? You're surrounded by a bunch of people who are just as fucked up as you are. The even better part? We lifted each other up. Just showing up was celebrated. Being able to talk in those sessions was celebrated. Not talking was supported. The littlest things were recognized as wins, because every teeny-tiny step moved you forward. It made my heart glad to be there.

Grappling with a mental health issue can be isolating, lonely, and downright sad. But when you can turn that around, it becomes something positive, bright, and hopeful. And sometimes? It can even be fun! Like the time a woman brought a coloring book to Group and started coloring while she listened. We were all curious, so she showed us what she was doing. The moderator thought it was a great idea, and soon people started asking for pages or borrowing her pencils and crayons. By the second week, most of us—men and women included—had our own books and either pencils or crayons. It kept the mood light and playful. There's definitely something to be said for art therapy and how it heals the soul.

I also started to take action outside of the hospital to work on myself. The same dear friend, Jenny, who had driven me to the hospital for my first intake, suggested I look into Co-Dependents Anonymous. Like Alcoholics Anonymous or Al-Anon, it's a 12-step program. But CoDA is for people who share a common desire to develop functional and healthy relationships.

When she first mentioned it, I was like, "What? Isn't that just for addicts?"

Boy, was I wrong.

I entered my first meeting a skeptic and left a believer. I had totally become co-dependent in my relationship with L.. I couldn't understand how. I had once been a strong, vibrant, independent woman capable of managing my life. And here I was, in a church basement, barely understanding why I had given up so much of myself for someone who couldn't match my energy. How did I let this happen?

The five core symptoms of codependency are:

✓ low self-esteem (check!)

✓ people-pleasing behaviors (check!)

✓ difficulty setting boundaries (check!)

✓ caretaking (reluctantly, but check!)

✓ dependency (check!)

Ding, ding, ding, ding, and ding.

Somehow, I had lost the fun-loving Nancy—Nan, Nanny, Nanny Goat, Nancy Fancy Pants, and Buffy (my nickname from my preppy days). The woman I used to be. And I needed to get her back. Pronto!

To investigate this further, I took off. Literally. I decided this was the perfect time to get out of Dodge and be by myself. So I booked a 12-day trip across the sea to the beautiful country of Croatia.

I had been to London and Paris before, but why Croatia? Frankly, despite its recent popularity from the filming of *Game of Thrones (GoT)*, it was because, many years ago, the actor Goran Visnjic from *ER* spoke so fondly of his homeland. I remember thinking how beautiful it sounded—and decided to just go.

I HIGHLY RECOMMEND THIS TO ANYONE. If you're ever given the chance to travel somewhere, do it. In the words of designer Christian Louboutin:

["Traveling makes you understand that you should not think that you are always right. You may think you know, but you don't."]

I used to travel a lot as a kid and in my early 20s. I loved it. I didn't go anywhere fancy, but it always made me feel capable. Back in the day, before Southwest and JetBlue, there was a small, low-cost airline called People's Express. You could often book roundtrip flights out of Newark Airport (before it was renamed Newark Liberty) for as little as $99. *Roundtrip!* I took full advantage of those rates and would fly to Cincinnati to visit my cousins, or hop down to Washington, D.C., or up to Boston. I don't think I ever thought twice about getting on a plane.

Of course, that changed after 9/11. Not only did I become nervous about what could happen if someone did something to the plane I was flying on, but I also worried that my nervousness would prevent me from helping my kids should something go wrong. One time, when my brother and I were flying down to our parents' winter home in Florida, we hit some bad turbulence. Since Rich and I were stay-at-home parents, we decided to take our kids to see their grandparents during winter break from school. The plane hit a pocket of turbulence so hard that the beverage cart crashed, and many of us screamed. That's when my fear of flying began. I tried to fly a few times afterward, but I was always in panic mode until we landed.

I pushed myself to fly to Croatia. I never wanted to do anything so badly in my life. Not even in my previous life, I don't think! Sure, I had wanted to get married and have kids—that was a given for me. But this? This was an adventure! This was bold! This was crazy! I was by myself, I didn't speak the language, and I was a single woman. What could possibly go wrong?

Well, aside from a last-minute plane change where my luggage got lost, everything went right. And I'd do it again in a wink. In fact, I love Croatia so much that I can talk about the country and its highlights *ad nauseam*. I'm sure I've bored many friends, family members, and even strangers with my stories. I don't care. It was the balm I needed at that moment, and it was delivered. And if the country ever has an opening for an ambassadorship—I will apply!

As my girlfriend Mary Ann called it, this was my *Eat, Pray, Croatia* journey. Unlike Elizabeth Gilbert, author of *Eat, Pray, Love*, however, I did not find love while on this voyage—yet it was there every step of the way. There is so much to learn about yourself when you travel.

For starters, when Swiss Air lost my suitcase (after assuring all of us on the connecting flight to Dubrovnik from Zurich that it *would not happen* because, "We're Swiss"—ha ha ha), I had to get a little creative with my beauty routine. My first night was at the gorgeous Hotel More, perched on a cliff above Lapad Bay in Dubrovnik. I had a two-bedroom, two-bath suite larger than most apartments and complete with a kitchen. Since I no longer had a brush, I pulled out a fork and used it to run through my hair after my shower. Hey, it worked. I looked human!

I also realized I needed to buy a few items to supplement what was in my overnight bag. The hotel staff suggested I take a bus to a nearby shopping center, and off I went. That was a little dicey because, as I mentioned, I didn't speak Croatian. I never like to play the "ugly American tourist," so I usually try to learn a few phrases in the host country's language. But I hadn't had the chance to do that before this trip. Fortunately, many Croatians speak English, and they are very kind.

As I walked to the bus stop, I marveled at the homes in the neighborhood. The architecture wasn't drastically different from American houses, but there were a few standout features. Case in point: one home had a *marble driveway*. Marble! Although that part of the country doesn't get snow, I'd think a surface like that would be extremely slippery when wet. Yikes!

Anyway, I got on the bus and told the driver the address the hotel manager had given me. He seemed to understand, nodded, and told me to find a seat. It was a Friday afternoon, I think, and the bus started to fill up. I began to get nervous because I wasn't hearing any stops being announced. A woman with a grandmotherly appearance got on, and I asked her if she knew the one I was looking for. She told me I had missed it.

I was about to get off at the last stop, along with everyone else, when the driver firmly told me to sit back down. He said he was going to circle around and start the route again. This was the only time I felt a little uneasy. Here I was—alone, on a bus, in a foreign country, with a driver who barely smiled and wasn't exactly exuding friendliness. Was he really going to help me... or kill me? I couldn't tell if he was friend or foe.

Thankfully, he was true to his word and got me back to the correct spot. What. A. Relief.

I don't know what kind of traveler you are, but I really enjoy exploring the differences of other cultures compared to my own. I don't like when things seem the same as where I'm from because to me, that's boring. Why would I want to see more of what I'm used to? Vive la difference! The more, the better, I say. And the shopping mall in downtown Dubrovnik did not disappoint — although it was nearly empty, like so many of its American counterparts are today. But I really enjoyed discovering all the different stores. One in particular stood out. It was a Benneton! If you don't know, Benneton is an Italian-based company, and growing up in the 80s, this brand was huge! Their tag line, "The United Colors of Benneton," resonated throughout the decade and into the next because their clothing was so bright, fun, and colorful. They embodied the neon lifestyle of that time. That day I picked up two shirts I still wear. I also found the Eastern European equivalent to Victoria's Secret, called Lisca. Although I wasn't looking for lingerie as the typical means to an end necessarily (nudge, nudge, wink, wink), I thought it was important to have more than one pair of underwear for this epic trip and heck, feeling pretty underneath your clothing is not a bad thing. Plus, I couldn't find a regular department store anywhere. I never did figure out where Croatians buy their Fruit of the Looms!

With my new gear in tow, and after checking on my missing bag with the hotel's manager, I settled into my one-night stand. I couldn't believe my tour operator had set me up in such a luxurious dwelling. The hotel had a bar built into a cave (it's famous for that), and my room had a large balcony overlooking the bay. The weather was so perfect that I decided to eat my small meal outside and enjoyed watching the buildings across the water light up as the night went on. I was extremely grateful to be there. It was as if my fairy godmothers knew I needed it at that time. I soaked it all up and prepared for my forthcoming adventure: the next day I would be leaving on a 7-day cruise in the Adriatic Sea.

As a kid, I would lie in my backyard, stare up at the sky, and watch planes go by. My parents' home was on a flight path for Newark Airport and there was frequent traffic. I loved imagining where all those lucky people were going and wondered what kind of adventures they were having without me. I knew someday I would join them, but never in a million years back then did I know I was going to be in this beautiful part of the world. I had only hoped.

Still without luggage, I headed down to the Dubrovnik harbor the next day. It was sunny and hot. As an August baby, I love the summer weather, and this fit the bill. I think my mind was still back in the United States though and hadn't gotten over the shock of being on this foreign soil. Regardless, I boarded the boat and met my Cruise Director, Harry. He was already aware of my lost bag and assured me it would be taken care of. As a seasoned travel professional and native Croatian, he had contacts in most of the ports we would be traveling in and out of and I felt confident he would get it delivered. I then settled into my spacious cabin. I was beginning to feel spoiled because first I had an apartment overlooking the water at the hotel and now I had a mini-suite on the water. There was a very large bathroom, a small sitting area, and a bed big enough for two people. I even had a porthole window. My tour operator definitely hooked me up.

A quick note about my cruising vessel: it is considered a small ship, and is a common way to tour the many ports along the Adriatic Sea, which is shallow. Larger cruise lines wouldn't be able to dock anywhere near the port cities. Because of this, there are very few passengers on board the smaller vessels. I believe the total for our trip was 48, with 38 passengers and about 10 crew members. As intimate as that is, my fellow travelers and I bustled about the first day as we found our cabins. We saved formal introductions for the Captain's Dinner that night.

Before we set sail, we were given the opportunity to explore the city of Dubrovnik. A little history lesson here, courtesy of my search engine: Croatia used to be a part of Yugoslavia. Prior to 1991, it was a socialist, one-party state made up of six republics: Bosnia and Herzegovina, Croatia, Macedonia, Montenegro, Serbia, and Slovenia. Its political composition was Marxist–Leninist from 1945–1948, then it was ruled by the "benevolent" dictator, Tito, from 1948–1990. From 1990–1991, Yugoslavia briefly became a multi-party state before dissolving, when Slovenia and Croatia declared their independence. If you remember any of this, you know that Serbia, under the leadership of the brutal dictator, Slobodan Milosevic, decided he wanted to keep those countries under his rule. This triggered a multi-ethnic war that would last until 1995.

The first point of interest we visited was Dubrovnik's old city, where we were given a walking tour of the walled area. *GoT* fans would recognize this as the setting for the famous scene in which Cersei Lannister is forced to walk naked through the streets as common folk pelt her with all sorts of things and shout, "Shame, shame, shame," as she walks by. We didn't see any unclothed people—after all, Croatia is a conservative, mostly Catholic country—but we did see many beautiful buildings, shops, restaurants, and landmarks, some of which date back to the Renaissance era. They are almost all made of limestone, the country's natural resource for building materials. It is quite majestic.

Our next stop was the Homeland War Museum, and it was very moving. Perched on top of a steep hill, it is located inside Fort Imperial. This magnificent limestone fortress on Srd Hill was originally construct-ed in 1812 by French soldiers from Napoleon the First's army during his Dalmatian Campaign. We had to take a cable car to the top, and the ride is not for the faint of heart, as it's a very, very high climb—1,352 feet. Despite the height, I enjoyed the magnificent views from the hilltop overlooking the Adriatic Sea. And as you look down at the walled city below, you can understand why it was considered as the setting for King's Landing in *GoT*.

Anyway, I had never been in a war-torn area before and can't imag-ine how people survived living through it all. The museum does an ex-cellent job of depicting this by showcasing photographs of the damage, displaying bullet-scarred objects, and playing news reports covering the horrific events. I believe about 130,000 people died in the conflicts that arose from Yugoslavia's dissolution. That is a large number of lives lost for such a small area. It is heartbreaking.

When we returned to our boat, we were given time to change and get ready for the Captain's Dinner, which was our first official meal. This is when I realized how utterly crazy I was for taking this trip, but also how lucky I was to be this brave—if that makes sense.

Before I left the U.S., I had asked my point person at the tour op-erator's office if I was the only single person on the cruise. She looked through her passenger list and responded that she wasn't 100% sure, but it did seem like there were a few others who were. What I should have asked instead was if I was the only solo traveler. Because, as it turns out, as part of our first night together, we were told to introduce ourselves, tell where we were from, and explain a little bit about why we were taking the cruise. Being the wallflower that I am, when it was my turn I'm sure I blurted out how I was newly divorced and traveling alone. The other single passengers? Well, they were part of a larger group of friends, mostly from Florida, who had decided to book the cruise together to celebrate their buddy's 40th birthday. They were a lot of fun and a great bunch of people. I even dubbed them "The Young Americans," and I'm happy to stay in touch with a few of them even now. But at that point in time, surrounded by them, a family of four, newlyweds, and many, many more couples, I felt alone. For about 10 minutes.

Standing vulnerable in front of all these strangers suddenly seemed empowering. I can't explain it; I just knew it was a privilege to be there on so many levels. My aura was starting to shift. I felt a confidence I hadn't had in years. And, coupled with the people around me and the positive experiences we had just shared, I began to feel joy—a joy that had been sorely missing from my life. So was peace. Forget leaving your heart in San Francisco, Tony—I left mine in Croatia.

Despite the August heat, the cruise was relaxing. The Adriatic waters are stunningly beautiful, and I can only remember one incident where we had rough water. Most of the time, the cruise was so smooth that it was hard to imagine we weren't riding on silk. Our itinerary was packed, but I never felt rushed. In addition to visiting these magical, medieval towns with castles, cathedrals, and walls of limestone everywhere, we had some really cool activities. During each stop, we had a tour of the area, which provided fascinating history and fun facts. For example, do you know why walls are curved in old towns? Well, that's to prevent splashback when drunken gentlemen leave a bar and can't make it home to empty their bladders in time. Seriously! Harry even assumed the pose for me in one of my pictures. I certainly can't easily erase that from my memories.

One of the most amazing places we visited was the Blue Grotto, or Blue Cave. I've never seen anything like it in person. It's off the coast of the island of Vis, and the water's color is other-worldly. Apparently, it gets the hue from the sunlight hitting the cave's limestone walls during certain times of the day. I caution that the trip is not for the claustro-phobic, as we had to duck down in our skip boat to make it through the entrance and exit. However, once you're inside, it is magnificent! Seeing it was definitely a once-in-a-lifetime experience.

Another side trip I was looking forward to was a family farm where they harvested mussels. Unfortunately, I had an accident on the way there. As I stepped forward toward the dock from our dinghy, it bobbed a little too forcefully, and my large right toe caught on the mooring line, ripping my toenail in half. The pain was excruciating. I can't describe it, but I can totally remember it. I was still able to enjoy a fabulous meal, but just barely, as my toe was throbbing. Fortunately, I was well taken care of by both the cruise staff and the friends I made on board.

A day after the incident, Harry took me to a clinic to have a doctor remove the damaged nail. What an interesting experience it was. The place seemed empty at first—neither patients nor staff could be found anywhere—but it was also incredibly cheap. I don't even know what kind of doctor performed the removal; I think she may have been a dermatologist! At that point, I didn't care because the pain had become unbearable, and the toe had started to bleed. Fortunately, Harry inter-preted for me, got the job done, and also negotiated a great deal so I only had to pay about $50 U.S. dollars for the procedure. Talk about dif-ferences—I'm sure if this had happened in the U.S., we would have sat in a crowded waiting room, and I would have paid at least $200. Have I mentioned yet how the Croatian people appear to be healthier than we are? This was a clear example of that fact.

Over the course of the voyage, I got to know more of my fellow passengers and was invited to hang out with them at times. Two couples from Australia were traveling together and had been friends for some time. They owned farms outside of Perth. I have the feeling that Australian farms are more like our ranches in middle America—wide open and encompassing hundreds, maybe even thousands, of acres. Regardless, Mark and Judy, and Lynley and Wayne, were kind to include me when dining on shore. And when I became injured, Mark, who had been an athletic trainer for rugby, wrapped my toe for me when I wanted to go swimming. It was little kindnesses like this that made my voyage very special.

The Young Americans—Kevin, Lori Ann, Julie, Josh, Jess, Bill, Michelle, Ryan, Whitney, Steve, Michael, and Chrissy—also contributed to my joyful travels. This group of friends was playful and fun. You could tell they enjoyed each other's company, and I was grateful to be included in their escapades as well. One night after dinner was especially memorable. Since many of the small ships travel the same route on the Adriatic Sea, it was not unusual for several boats to dock together in the same port. Legend has it that the captains race each other to get to port first, in order to get the best spot on the dock. If that's true, then our captain did a great job, as we always seemed to be first in line. But at least once or twice, we had to cross through the other boats to get to ours. While doing this, we became familiar with passengers from the other vessels. There was one group of men, mostly from New York City, who were traveling together to also celebrate their friend's birthday. Their hosts, a married couple, had charted the entire ship for the week and invited as many friends as they could fit on the cruise to come along.

That's how we met Jonathan. He had been invited to cruise with the New Yorkers but decided he wanted a break from their partying ways, especially after their boat was kicked out of one of the ports for being too loud! To escape their capers, he joined the YAs and me a few times. It turns out that Jonathan had performed as a professional singer, and after one dinner, as our large group walked the cobbled streets, we came upon a young man playing guitar outside a small café. He was really good, and we decided to stop and listen. When we discovered he took requests, Jonathan asked him to play Whitney Houston's "I Wanna Dance with Somebody" and sang along beautifully. We all eventually joined in, including the other café patrons. For me, it was a magical moment. Here we were, sharing an experience in this old, old city, in beautiful surroundings, laughing and singing with total strangers. I didn't have anyone critiquing my behavior or hurrying me to move along. I could just be. Do you know how the experts say we should be present in the moment? That was one of many times it happened for me on this trip.

Other moments like this happened when I went about exploring on my own. Like when Harry told us that a movie was being shown in a local park one night. It was Quentin Tarantino's *Once Upon a Time in Hollywood,* and it was a thrill to sit and watch Leonardo DiCaprio and Brad Pitt speak in English with Croatian subtitles. I was a little nervous at first to attend because I was on my own and, up until that point, had gotten away with speaking English during most interactions in shops and restaurants. This time, however, I was among the general population, standing in line for a popular event. They were planning to close the gates because all seats were filled, but there was still a large line of people waiting to get in. Fortunately for me, I struck up a conversation with a few young girls who took pity on me, and they begged the gatekeeper to let me in with them. We made it just in time and sat on a garden wall beneath a large tree. The night was so calm, and the air seemed perfect, as it had cooled down from the day. I felt very lucky and grateful to be there—even as I watched Margaret Qualley's face melt. Eww. Have I mentioned that having three brothers contributed to my twisted sense of humor?

My new friends from the ship and I parted company when the cruise ended in the city of Split. I had a few more days left of my solo trip and was whisked away by a friendly young man assigned to me by my tour operator. His nickname was Andy, and like Harry, he had been in the travel business for a few years. Andy's job was to drive me for over two hours to the interior of Croatia. Along the way, we talked about our different countries, a business idea he had, and life in general. When he noticed I was nodding off, he graciously suggested a stop for coffee, where the roadside attraction included a beautiful Russian brown bear. I guess I needed to stretch my legs.

Our destination was one of Croatia's oldest national parks, Plitvice Lakes. It is a UNESCO World Heritage Site, rightly so, and is simply breathtaking. Look it up and see for yourself. There are majestic water-falls around every corner. It looks as if an AI dreamscape came to life. Before the cruise ended and as I was preparing for my solo journey, I had asked Harry if, as a single woman traveling alone, I would be safe walking around the park by myself. I had visited several in the U.S. with L. and the kids and pictured this to be similar – a wide open, vast landscape with no one around except some wildlife. Harry gave a little scoff-like laugh and told me I would be fine. It turned out he was correct because there is a boardwalk you use to meander the entire perimeter of the area, and it was crowded with tourists. I never felt I was in danger.

The landscape of this part of Croatia was a stark contrast to the villages and port cities we visited on the cruise. In fact, it reminded me of Canada and the northeastern United States like Maine, New Hampshire, or Vermont. It is even similar to the Adirondacks in upstate New York where L. insisted we take our vacations every summer since that is what he did as a child. It was dark and foresty (aren't all forests dark?), and the hotel was alpine style, reminding me of pictures I had seen of Austria, Germany, and Switzerland. I was only there for one night, and after being overstimulated by the explosion of scenery in the park, I enjoyed a swim in the pool and ate a wonderful meal in the hotel's attached restaurant. It is called peka (p-eh-ka) and is considered a national dish of the country. Although it can be served with either meat or seafood, this meal was wisely served with meat, being that we were nowhere near the sea. And boy, was it delicious! I can recall its savory taste to this day. It is a wonder I didn't gain weight on my holiday because I didn't turn down a single meal. I'm just not a polite eater. I like food, a lot, and I wanted the opportunity to try something different. I'm glad I did.

On to the Istrian Peninsula the next day and my hotel in Opatija. The land is shared by the three countries of Serbia, Croatia, and Italy. This part of Croatia is considered the poshest and is referred to as the country's Riviera. It is no surprise, as you could tell the shops, restaurants, and hotels cater to a clientele above my pay grade. But I love pretending I'm part of the world's 1%! Pretending decreases my responsibility to maintaining the global economy. Although throughout this journey, I did stay in beautiful hotels and was chauffeured around by handsome men in luxury cars. I felt very spoiled. My money was extremely well spent on this trip.

It was during this time I had another chance to stop and contemplate. I had finished my dinner and was walking around a park. The weather was perfect once again. Not oppressively hot; just comfortable. I stopped to sit on a bench and looked around. There was a light breeze rustling the leaves of the trees. It was so peaceful that I felt calm and reflective. I thought to myself: I'm alive. A year earlier, I did not think I would make it through all the pain and drama my divorce turned into. Yet I survived it. Not only that, I was also currently sitting in a beautiful part of the world enjoying the hell out of my adventures. Deep down, I figured that as long as L. remained in my life, there would be more unhappy times down the road since he had a singular goal of making my life as difficult as possible. But for that moment in time, I relished the feeling of power and strength I was now tasting.

Shortly thereafter, I heard a band strike up music behind me. I believe the locals were celebrating a holiday and the band was playing to mark the occasion. Many people stopped to listen, and some dancers joined in. It was really lively and lovely. For all I knew, this could have been a regular occurrence for a Saturday summer night in Opatija. I didn't care because it was special to me—as if these folks were sending me back to America with all the positive vibes their music and dancing could give me, and I took it and ran with it.

I think the only disappointment about my trip was a minor one. I haven't had a "Bucket List" since I developed my fear of flying, but when I did have one, Venice, Italy, was on it. And since Croatia shares the Istrian Peninsula with Italy, I was sure I would be able to sneak over the border and get to see the famed city. Unfortunately, I ran out of time because I had to get back to my daughter, who was about to start her senior year of high school. Alas, the only thing I was able to see of Venice was their airport, which didn't disappoint. After all, how many times have you seen, much less set foot in, a Ferrari store? I not only walked in but shortly walked out when I realized I would never, ever own one of those cars. Too bad. They look fun to drive.

A month after I returned from my trip, I also threw myself a divorce party to celebrate my newfound freedom. I wanted to continue adding joy to my life, and this was one way to do it, in my opinion. My college drinking shenanigans aside, I loved throwing parties as a way to express my appreciation for friends and family. Unfortunately, this was another aspect of my personality I had diminished for my spouse's sake, who wasn't as engaging as me. I went all out renting a tent, having it catered, hiring a DJ, and having my brother's friend's band play. It was an amazing, happy occasion as many family, friends, and neighbors partied with me. My light was beginning to grow brighter, and I was glad about it.

6

The Circle of Hell
Dante Forgot

I have a dear friend, Stacey, who met her husband, David, through an online dating app. In fact, they are part of that company's marketing campaign because A) their story is so damn cute, and B) they are both actors and models and therefore, pretty damn good-looking. However, I hate to break it to anyone else entering the fray—unless you know how to market yourself, and it is ALL about marketing—your chances of meeting and finding true love online are very, very slim.

Yet, I found the process to be super fun. I truly did! I only dated one guy briefly when I was in high school, had gotten into a few situation-ships in college, and had one serious relationship before I met L. So on-line dating was my candy store. I was able to meet many different men of all shapes, colors, ages, and backgrounds, and enjoyed their company as I learned how to navigate this process at the tender age of 54. There were only a few I dated more than once; most didn't make the grade, either on my part or theirs. There were a lot of nice men and there were some jerks as well. There were even some who were just odd. The

BEST story I have from these escapades is this: I connected with a man who looked a lot like Cody from the TLC show *Sister Wives*, and we hit it off conversationally through text. We spoke at least once on the phone, and he suggested we meet in person. Since he lived almost an hour away, he thought a good place would be my local Sam's Club, since he was planning to run some errands there anyway.

Well, it was a hot summer day, and I had my car's A/C cranked. I was just pulling into the parking lot when he texted and asked where I was. I was about one minute late, I kid you not, and since I always run behind, I was proud of myself for making it on time! Anyway, he texted back that he was standing inside the door to keep cool. I understood. I did not understand, however, what happened next. We said an awkward "Hello," and hugged, and then he said, "Well, let's grab a shopping cart. I have to buy some water for my kids." Excuse me, WHAT? This was our first date? Yes, this was our first date. I couldn't help but point out how unusual this was. He did not seem amused. In fact, he did not seem to crack a smile or joke about anything. He added to that lack of joviality when I mistakenly asked which sport his kids played, and he barked back, "I already told you!" Should I have run then and there? Probably! But no, I decided to give him the benefit of the doubt and continued our adventures at a nice restaurant around the corner.

Lunch was not much better. Conversation was somewhat strained, and I knew this wasn't going anywhere. But ever the hapless romantic, I thought a second date might be a good idea. I don't know why, other than to see if we got off on the wrong foot. He obviously didn't feel the same way, and as we parted company in the parking lot, I remembered I hadn't asked him his last name and said something to that effect. He responded with a rushed, "Oh, I'll text it to you," and I laughed to myself as I got in my car because I knew that wasn't going to happen. It didn't. The best part about that situation, though, has been the retelling of it.

It makes me and anyone who's heard it laugh because it was so bizarre. Thank you, Sir Cody, for that!

Most of the time, the dates were a nice way to get to know someone better, and my old journalism instincts made it comfortable to ask questions. It was definitely easier to do that in person, and going offline for an actual date was generally the goal. But then there was the one guy who didn't even get out of the gate when he told me, during our telephone exchange, how he and his ex-wife had "porno sex," and just let it hang in the air. I don't remember my exact response, but I'm sure it was along the lines of, "How nice for you." As soon as I was able to, I wrote my daughter a quick note asking her to interrupt our conversation so that I could quickly hang up. Seriously, men, this is your competition.

I also tried using a matchmaker and found it to be just as bad. These romance agencies are anything but. The process went something like this: I made an appointment with a dating agency that was advertised by their "good friend," a local radio personality. I had an extensive in-person interview and filled out a few questionnaires. I had a nice rapport with the young woman whom I met with. She took a casual picture of me, claiming it was just for their files. It was pretty awful, I have to say, but they didn't really prepare me. Anyway, when it came down to what I was looking for in a partner, I recall saying I had a few specific requirements: 1) someone college-educated, 2) someone older and taller than me, and 3) someone with kids. Pretty vague but simple, if you ask me. I was looking forward to these cupid-adjacent women working their magic for me, but they never delivered. For example, my first date was with a nice-enough looking guy, not college-educated, and didn't have kids. He mentioned how he had used their services for several years (several or 7, I can't recall exactly, but that's 6 too many) and was as surprised as I was that they set him up with me, because apparently, I wasn't his type. I never did ask him what that was, because I didn't care. The date ended painlessly enough, yet I contacted the agency soon after to ask why they matched me with someone who clearly didn't meet the requirements they had asked me to provide. After all, I paid them a hefty fee for the luxury of 4 dates. They apologized and said they'd do better. They did not. What a waste of my time and money. I totally don't recommend that route to anyone.

At the same time as I was dipping my toe into the dating pool, I stumbled upon a Facebook ad for what looked like a very interesting course called, "Find the Right-1™" (FTR-1™) Fresh off my match-making disaster, I did not want to repeat the same financial mistake, but something about the dapper man in the picture intrigued me. I quickly learned that this gentleman, Eli Schostak, was a former therapist who had taken his own years of dating experience, as well as those of former clients, and developed a system to "help singles get into and grow healthy relationships."

I had always thought that self-love was selfish and, frankly, gross, since I associated loving oneself with auto-erotica. After all, that type of behavior is strictly forbidden in the Catholic Church. They beat your head with a stick (figuratively) about sex in general, since its main purpose is for procreation. So pre-marital sex, self-pleasure, and anything good about intercourse is a big No-No. After all, you're not supposed to enjoy it, God forbid! You're just supposed to make babies. Sheesh! I totally failed to understand that part.

Anyway, I had a lot to learn about what self-love really was. I can't exactly explain how he did it (it's proprietary information, after all), but simply put, Eli showed his students how, when you believe that love of self is only created when others love you, then that is where you're going to get screwed up. In other words, YOU HAVE TO LOVE YOUR-SELF FIRST BEFORE ANYONE ELSE CAN LOVE YOU. I'm sure you've heard this before, and I did too. But how many of us put this into practice? Especially women? This was my "A-ha!" moment. Going through the steps of FTR-1 ™ helped me reframe my thoughts about myself, first and foremost, and then how I could apply that newfound knowledge to my other relationships. It isn't only about dating – I mean, these simple principles apply to how you interact with just about anyone. Basically, once I learned to change my perspective, I started to approach not only dating differently but LIFE! Don't get me wrong—it's a process that takes time. But once you take the right steps for you, it makes things easier. I wanted to be loved in a healthy way. I deserve to be loved in a healthy way. We all do.

So essentially, by taking FTR-1™, I finally met the love of my life for the first time. I'm sure it sounds completely corny, but it is totally true. Once I started putting myself first in my life—not in a selfish way, but in a balanced way—my life changed for the better, and eventually, I was healthy enough to meet and fall in love with the man of my dreams. More about him later!

Armed with this new and revealing information, I had to learn new habits about how to treat myself. The trip overseas and my post-divorce party celebration were just the beginning. And let me stop here to acknowledge something: I am privileged. I know it. Not every woman going through a divorce can do what I have done. I am extremely lucky and fortunate. Even blessed, if you want to go there. I have many friends who did not land on their feet after their divorces, and it's heartbreaking. I have held their hands as they have tried to piece their lives back together. My situation was different because of two facts: if I had made the first move, L.'s ego would have prevented him from being cooperative. I believe in my heart his guilt worked in my financial favor. I also happened to have an excellent, excellent lawyer who saw how broken I was and decided the best course of action would be for me to get away from him as best as could be. She proposed a lump sum settlement, where I received alimony in one payment, as opposed to having it delivered monthly for years. She even shielded me from his attacks as they grew stronger during our "conscious uncoupling." For example, she made sure there was always a buffer by putting us in separate rooms when it came time for mediation or handling most communications between the two of us. She was so protective of me that I affectionately gave her the nickname of "Bulldog," because she's that fierce. Plus, she's tiny! Her support saved my life in a significant way. Thank you, Diana.

If you're able to do any of the things I did—great! But that is not the point of my story. I'm sharing mine to get you to realize that EVEN SMALL STEPS MAKE A DIFFERENCE! Take a bath, read a book, plant a garden, etc. Take time for you! Don't let YOU get lost. I used to scoff at women who regularly got manicures because I thought it was selfish. It is not! We all need to do things to balance ourselves in our everyday lives, whether we are going through a divorce or not. And in a healthy relationship, your significant other does not criticize you for doing the things that help you keep that balance. Or, in my case, pressure you to do things for them. In fact, they may encourage you to do things for yourself or even join in your adventures!

Have you ever seen *The Runaway Bride*? I know, it's another reference to another Julia Roberts movie, but the part where Richard Gere calls out Julia Roberts' character, Maggie, on not knowing what she wants out of life, really resonated with me and kept replaying over and over in my head as my life unfolded. It goes something like this: Gere plays Ike, a journalist who's planning to expose Maggie as an erratic woman for leaving many men at the altar. After interviewing her and her different jilted victims, Ike notices that when she's with each man, she claims to like the kinds of egg dishes that those men like. He then asks Maggie how she prefers her eggs. It gets her thinking, and she sets off on a journey of self-discovery.

Many people also told me that post-divorce was the time for me to figure out what I wanted to do with my life. I thought about it more like: who I wanted to be when I grew up. And that scared me. I mean, I was initially afraid I wouldn't be able to handle things on my own, despite knowing I wasn't on my own since I had friends and family for support and had done this (living by myself) thing before. It was more than that. Through therapy, I discovered my big fear was success. I think it always has been. After all, I knew what it was like to fail. Failed career choices, failed relationships; it's a familiar feeling. But success? I never tasted that before! And now I had freedom, and I was the only one holding me back. What was I to do about it all? I decided it was time to scare the shit out of myself by trying new things and dove headfirst into anything that was going to make me feel good – regardless of the outcome.

First things first. I signed up for Bartending School. Why would that scare anyone? Well, you see, one of the unfortunate side effects of being on Lithium can be hand tremors, and it happened to me. My hands already have a natural shake to them, which increases with nervousness or stress. I tried to hide it as best as I could while dating, but it wasn't always easy. I remember at least one prospect asking why I hadn't touched my drink during our date. It was embarrassing! But I thought this experience would be fun, and I had always wanted to learn how to mix the perfect drink. And it was fun! We had a small class of about six students, and our teacher was a former restaurateur. He gave us a lot of good information, was very amusing at times, and seemed sympathetic to my condition. At least I think so. To say he was a little shocked at my hands flying all over the place as I attempted to make my first drink would be mild. His eyes widened to saucer size, and he asked what was going on. I quickly explained how my medication contributed to my jazz hands and added that he needn't worry because I had no illusions of becoming a professional mixologist. I enjoyed the classes and appreciated getting out of the house and meeting new people. Unfortunately, I didn't retain much of the information imparted to us, but I did become an expert at the shaken, not stirred martini!

I also signed up for a stand-up comedy class as another way to scare myself out of my comfort zone. I had attempted it once before when my son had just been born. Back then, I signed up for a class that a local comedian (who is also a lawyer and was a Councilman, because what's funnier than those two professions, right?) offered through an Adult Education program. I thought it would help me improve my writing or be a way to help me find my comedic voice. I didn't expect to perform at the end of the course. I should have read the syllabus. I initially didn't want to tell L. what the class was, because I didn't want him criticizing me for wasting time. When I finally did inform him, his reaction was along those lines. More or less, he told me he wouldn't watch me perform because he didn't want to see me embarrass myself. I think he meant him. Of course, he meant him. Regardless, I persevered. Sort of.

A few friends from work—Bev, Carol, Lori, Joe, and Mark—showed up to support me the night of our show. I had practiced a few lines of amusing material, but I decided the only way I could manage my out-of-control nerves was to sing a song my mother would recite to me as a kid. I originally thought it was a lullaby since she had such a sweet voice. When I asked her if she remembered the name of the cradle tune, she laughed and told me it was a drinking song she learned in college! Needless to say, that fact was incorporated into my 5-minute comedy debut before I launched into the song. My teacher was not pleased with my decision, but it was either do that or wither off the stage. I wanted to save face, and since the lyrics are about drunken circumstances, I figured it would at least get a chuckle. It did.

My second time on stage was completely different. When I signed up for my second stand-up comedy class, I was fresh out of the hospital, freshly diagnosed with a mental health disorder, and ready to turn the world on its head about what it means to have suicidal intentions. That's right, I performed a stand-up routine comparing suicide to erectile dysfunction. True story. Well, not exactly, but close.

As I said earlier, I was desperately seeking solace during this time of duress. The more I got out of the house and did things, the better I felt. In fact, I was so often in my car that my brother, Rich, jokingly said I should just live out of it. It wasn't because I couldn't sit still; it's just that I didn't want to be alone with my bad thoughts and feelings. Call it escapism, but it's what I needed at the time, and it worked for me.

Don't ask me how I ended up in a comedy class, though. It was probably due to surfing the Internet for something else when I came across an advertisement for ArtsQuest, the cultural center of the Lehigh Valley in eastern Pennsylvania. I was still living in New Jersey at this point, but when I discovered all of these fun classes were being offered within driving distance, I couldn't resist looking at what they had. They have several art classes, like glass-blowing, photography, ceramics, and jewelry making, to name a few, but those weren't going to cut it for me. Lo and behold, when I saw the information for improv and stand-up classes, I was intrigued. I asked myself (I'm guessing it was figuratively, but it could have been literally as I've been known to talk to myself, especially in grocery stores): Could I try this again? It was fun the first time, so why not? What did I have to lose?

On our first day of class, we were asked to stand up in front and introduce ourselves, giving a brief explanation of why we were taking the course. The place was packed! I think there were over 20 students of various stages and ages. One classmate claimed she had no recollection of signing up but found the charge on her credit card statement and figured she must've booked it during a personal wine fest. That struck a nerve with me, so when it was my turn, I announced that I had *suicide-ordered* my class. I got both a gasp and a laugh—so I knew I was onto something.

I began shaping my routine around the idea that we should be able to talk about suicide—although we rarely do. I was hell-bent on breaking the stigma that surrounds mental illness. I still am, which is one reason I'm so open about sharing my story and discussing this subject with anyone and everyone. It's a hard topic, yes, but keeping your feelings in can destroy you. I've seen it happen too many times. I also believe it was a major contributor to the failure of my marriage—on both sides. Among other things.

Our comedy class instructors, Ryan and Ja Near, were seasoned comedians whose expertise helped us fine-tune our material. They added nuances that made our lines stronger and taught us some time-tested techniques, like using the *rule of threes*. Basically, if you're writing humorous content with a list of three things, the funny part should come last—usually something surprising, shocking, or the opposite of what the audience expects (also known as a *reversal*). Comedy thrives on the unexpected. An example would be: "Three animals walk into a bar—a dog, a cat, and a fish. The dog says, 'I'd like a bone, please.' The cat says, 'I'd like a bowl of milk, please.' And the fish says, 'Give me a beer.'" (Were you expecting the fish to ask for a glass of water? Ok, so I'm not a comic genius like Brad Williams.)

Unfortunately, COVID struck during our class, and it was put on hold while we all hunkered down at home. When we reemerged, Ryan got in touch and told us we were still welcome to perform. After all, we had paid for the class, and he wanted to give us the opportunity to see it through. Out of all the original students, only three of us ultimately agreed to go ahead.

When the day arrived to perform our routines in front of a small audience of friends and family, I nearly puked. My heart pounded so hard my chest hurt, and my breathing was rapid. I hadn't memorized my material, and with the help of the Lithium I was taking, my hands— and my entire body—shook like salt and pepper shakers seasoning your favorite dish. Knowing this would probably happen, I worked it into my routine. Ryan even suggested I compare my flapping hands to an ostrich, which I did—and it got a cute laugh.

Unlike my first attempt at stand-up, this time I pushed through and performed the material I had written instead of singing a silly song. The video of my performance is painful for me to watch now. Awful, really. Not because the material wasn't good—I had some solid jokes!—but because I was so beyond scared, I just read everything off the little card next to me. I know my timing would've been better if I could've held it together. Next time, I'm taking the Ativan I use for my fear of flying. Lots of it.

Ultimately, though, I'm really glad I performed—and proud of myself for persevering. My performance wasn't polished, and it wasn't elegant, but I said what I wanted to say and got my message across: we shouldn't be afraid to talk about hard, dark subjects like suicide. Bringing it into the light helps destroy the shame surrounding it. I want to keep doing that. And I will.

Well, following that monumental brush with stage fright, I, of course, had to find another way to explore what I want to be when I grow up. There was a workshop being offered online by a well-established podcaster, so I decided to take it. After all, there's something freeing about interviewing people without having to worry about your visual image.

And although podcasting has transformed into a visual medium for some, I prefer the old-fashioned, talk-radio format. It's cozy and more intimate when it's stripped down to just a few people talking to each other. In my humble opinion.

The main goal of taking the class wasn't just to learn a new skill—which I did—but to also challenge myself to create something on my own. I did it just for me. I didn't care how many listeners I had because I was having fun doing it. It brought me back to my original dream of being a journalist, or hosting my own talk show like Barbara Walters or Rona Barrett did in the '70s and '80s.

My original idea was to host a show in which guests would talk about a mistake they made and what they learned from it. It was called *You Did What?!* and I produced 12 episodes. They're quite rudimentary because I didn't edit any of them—and you can tell. I was so eager to try things out I didn't want to waste time taking that extra step. Overall, I think they sound pretty good, except for one where my guest kept cutting in and out. I later learned it's better to interview using computer software instead of over the phone. Most of the time, the sound quality is better that way.

All my guests were friends, family members, or classmates. Their topics ranged from humorous to serious. For example, I asked my little brother, George, and his friend, Kurt, to recount the time they held a drag race down a steep hill, which ended with Kurt flipping his car onto the lawn of our local funeral home. Obviously, Kurt survived—and they both learned not to be so reckless. Kurt went a step further and decided to drive "like a grandma" from that point on. He claims he still does.

Another guest was a classmate from the workshop, MB Marshall Lee. In her episode, we discussed the role of self-advocacy in health care—whether for your physical or mental well-being. Through her own podcast, *My Season, Your Reason*, MB has become a passionate warrior on a mission to educate the African-American community in her native Washington, D.C., about the positive impact communication can have when speaking to healthcare providers—for yourself or on behalf of a loved one.

Over the four months of this project, my guests and I shared many important insights, including having no regrets, treating others with respect, and just living life. We also reflected on life paths and the lessons we've learned along the way. Most importantly, we learned to never teach your dog how to ring a doorbell. Seriously—it's a thing. Look it up, or listen to Episode 9: *"Don't Ever Teach Your Dog How to Ring a Doorbell!"*

Not only did I strengthen my relationships with those who participated in this little endeavor, but I also formed lasting friendships with other podcasters from the U.S., Canada, and Australia. I really enjoyed it. However, it didn't quite work the way I had hoped. It was difficult to find guests who were willing to talk about their mistakes. That was eye-opening for me. I find it freeing—and even educational—to talk openly about my missteps, whether in an intimate setting or over the airwaves. Others don't always feel the same. Some were reluctant to air their dirty laundry, even when I assured them I had very few listeners. Convincing friends and family to be on the show was harder than expected.

But I'm not giving up. With encouragement from my career coach, Iky Chan, and my podcasting coach, Steph Thompson, I plan to re-launch the show after the publication of this book. There will be a new title, a new logo, and fresh subject material. Stay tuned!

All the time I spent taking classes, workshops, and programs was building toward something bigger. I just didn't know what it was at the time.

I eventually found out.

7

My "Meet Cute" Love Story

I had never heard the term "meet cute" until I watched what is now one of my favorite movies, *The Holiday*, starring Kate Winslet, Cameron Diaz, Jude Law, and Jack Black. In short, it's a sappy rom-com in which the two female protagonists switch homes due to romances gone awry. Winslet swaps her charming English cottage for Diaz's modern LA abode, and both find true love in the process—Winslet with the charming Black, and Diaz with the moody Law.

Along the way, Winslet's character also befriends an elderly gentleman who is a screenwriter, played by one of the great supporting actors, Eli Wallach. In this role, he teaches her how a first encounter between characters can lead to a romantic relationship if the experience is playful, sweet, charming—or even just pleasant. I would have to say that meeting my boyfriend was all of the above.

I wasn't looking for a relationship when we crossed paths because I had decided to give online dating a break and concentrate on hanging out with friends. I had signed up for a women's social network, and one of the members, Heidi, posted that she was going to host a Super Bowl viewing party at a local brewery and asked if anyone wanted to join her. I LOVE football, and since my ex didn't, we never really watched it. I immediately said yes, and when I mentioned it to my girlfriend, Nisi Isabella, she decided to join us as well.

I met Heidi first, then another young lady joined us. Nisi arrived after work, and the four of us sat in front of the big screen. When we realized the other patrons weren't really paying attention to the game like we were—and Nisi got hungry—I asked Heidi if there was somewhere else we could go to get food and enjoy the game. She mentioned there was a place around the corner, and we followed her over there.

When we walked into that bar, I couldn't believe it—I felt as if I had found my *Cheers*. There were middle-aged people everywhere, laughing, dancing, and just having fun! And quite a few of them seemed to know each other. It was all very friendly. How did I not know this existed? It was amazing.

I struck up a conversation with Tim, who told me the patrons were mostly part of a group called "Sunday Funday," and they gathered to watch football, throw parties, and attend live music events together. It looked like a great bunch of folks, and he mentioned that if I wanted to join them, I could ask the administrator on Facebook to add me to their list so I'd be notified of upcoming events.

He also pointed out how there was a fundraiser going on at the same time for a local charity. They were collecting for a 50/50 raffle as well as selling t-shirts. The charity provides free clothing and toiletries to the homeless throughout Pennsylvania's Lehigh Valley. Since I was looking for a volunteer opportunity, I thought I'd ask if they needed help.

I decided to approach this nice-looking man, Mel, who was wearing the organization's shirt, and asked him about their work. He happened to have the most beautiful blue eyes, nice hair, and a great smile. Plus, he smelled really, really good. He was very sweet, too, and we spent a few minutes discussing his friend's charity. When I mentioned wanting to volunteer, he gave me her business card, and I told him I'd probably call her that week to meet in person.

Little did I know that chance encounter was about to change my life.

This handsome, kind gentleman left a great impression on me, and when I got home, I quickly did two things: I asked to join the "Sunday Funday" group, and once I was admitted, I stalked him on Facebook. Seriously! I mean, a girl has to find out if a prospective suitor has potential—and most of all, that he's not married, right?

I'm so glad I did, because he had recently posted about his eldest daughter's engagement, and it was written with such love that I couldn't help but feel there was something special about him. I had the sense that getting to know him would be worth it. My intuition whispered he might even be the family man I was looking for.

Since we hadn't exchanged phone numbers, I wasn't sure how we'd ever cross paths again. Unbeknownst to me, he felt the same way and decided to do something clever to get my attention. He bought a ticket for me to attend his friend's next charity event and asked her to give it to me when I met with her to discuss volunteering. He even included his phone number, just in case I wanted to call and thank him.

Unfortunately, she didn't give me the ticket when we met, and another week passed. I kept thinking about him, wondering if he was all I imagined. Since I couldn't get him off my mind, I decided to take action and went back to the scene of the crime—twice!

The first time, my friend, Maria, and I went out for drinks. We stopped at a bar that turned out to be a hotspot for the local college crowd. We quickly left, feeling old and out of place. I then took her to the pub where I had met Mel, thinking we'd feel more comfortable there—and yes, secretly hoping he'd also be there. But it was extremely empty that night, and once again, no Mel.

Another week went by. This time, another friend, Lee, wanted to go out with her boyfriend. I could've suggested other places, but I figured the third time might be the charm. Off we went to the same pub. We were sitting at the bar, enjoying our drinks and conversation. The place was crowded and loud this time.

I excused myself to go to the ladies' room, and when I came out—there he was. I couldn't believe it. I hesitated. Should I be bold and walk up to him? Would he even remember me? I took a breath and moved forward, heart pounding. I tapped Mel on the shoulder, and he turned around.

Any doubt about how he felt quickly vanished. His jaw practically dropped when he saw me. I smiled and said, "Hi Mel! Do you remember me?" He almost sputtered as he replied, "Do I remember you? Of course I do!"

He asked if I was there with anyone, and when I mentioned my friend and her boyfriend, he promptly joined us—and didn't leave my side the rest of the night. He quickly made friends with my friends, and as the evening went on, several of his friends came over to chat too.

Now, a little note about Mel: he's an introvert but very outgoing. I know that sounds like a contradiction, but he told me that when he was young, he made the decision to come out of his shell so he could have a social life. I admitted I did the same. I remember reading an article in

Seventeen magazine when I was a teen called "How Not to Be a Wallflower." Maybe that's why we clicked.

Regardless, things began falling into place. Several of his friends—many of them women—came over and extolled his virtues. It was remarkable. Lee and I gave each other that, "What the heck is going on?" look.

It wasn't just one or two women—about ten of them kept telling me how sweet, kind, and wonderful he was. The best line came from his friend, Kim, who said, "If you break his heart, I will break your face." I instantly fell in love with her for that fierce loyalty and the sheer balls it took to say that to a total stranger. To this day, I consider her one strong motherfucker—and now, a great friend.

But to say my relationship with Mel was smooth sailing from the start wouldn't be true.

I had learned in my FTR-1™ class that we can fall into "rabbit holes" in our relationships. I had identified mine and learned how to climb out if I recognized the signs.

A perfect example? An incident Mel and I call "The Blip," which happened during our first few weeks of going out.

Before I began dating again, I read *The Secret* and watched the movie of the same name. If you're unfamiliar, it's basically a guide to manifesting anything you want into your life. It is a spiritual practice called The Law of Attraction, which says that what you put out into the universe will come back to you.

So, if you want to attract the perfect partner, you write down everything you want in them: likes, dislikes, values, hobbies, family dynamics—at least 100 points.

Mel came closer than anyone I've ever dated (or married) to meeting that list. But it was hard for me to trust his sincerity.

That was my rabbit hole.

At the time our relationship was budding, I was also working with a therapist I like to describe as an energy healer. Angela B. approached counseling differently. Instead of the usual, "How does that make you feel?" she suggested affirmations, prayers, and meditation. For example, when I presented problems to her, she would listen and then offer feedback that helped me see things in a way that connected with my spirituality and aligned with the Law of Attraction.

As a polytheist, I prefer to refer to the higher power as "Holy Spirit" rather than God—because I feel it's arrogant of us to assume we know his/her/its name. Angela B. was very respectful of that. Some of the phrases she gave me to use included: *"I am open, ready, and allow miracles like love or unconditional love into my life," "I allow the Holy Spirit to work on my behalf,"* and *"I allow, I accept, and I am ready to receive."* These affirmations played an important role in what happened between Mel and me.

I think the biggest compliment (of many) I can give my handsome boyfriend is the same thing I once said about my mom: he's not perfect, but he loves me perfectly. He has the biggest heart. And sometimes, it gets in the way.

He's sweetly old-fashioned and insisted on paying for everything whenever we went out. I offered at times—he appreciated it, but would decline. He also presented me with small gifts and other tokens of affection like flowers and candy. Don't get me wrong—I really enjoyed being spoiled this way, especially because it had been so long since I'd been shown that kind of affection. But after two incidents, it started to feel a little uncomfortable.

The first was during a garden show we attended together. As we perused the vendors' stalls, I noticed a cute cement elephant statue and thought it would make a nice gift for my daughter, since elephants are her favorite animal. But I thought it was too expensive and decided not to purchase it. I also passed on a smaller cement elephant pot. Mel noticed my hesitation and took it upon himself to buy them for me. He excused himself, said he had to use the Men's Room, and then came walking back with both items in his hands. I wasn't happy. I felt like he had undermined my decision, but I didn't say anything then. I took it as a kind gesture and accepted the gifts.

The second incident made me uncomfortable in a different way.

Another class I signed up for post-divorce (yes, ANOTHER class! I was working hard at finding myself. Get over it.) was for voiceover acting. I've been interested in that field ever since my sophomore year of high school, when my history teacher, Sr. Marion Wagner, challenged our class to read a long passage aloud, one at a time. We all sucked at first, so she had us do it again. I purposely slowed down, paused at the commas, put feeling into it—and won the competition. Ever since, reading aloud has been one of my favorite things. But I digress!

So I signed up for this voiceover class at my local community college. It was a one-day, three-hour session. Being new to the area and unfamiliar with the campus, I got lost. Super lost. I was running nearly an hour late. In a panic, I called Mel to ask what I should do—bag the class or keep trying to find it? He suggested I forge ahead since I had already paid for it and because discovering more about this topic was important to me.

I took his advice, eventually found the room, and enjoyed the remainder of the class, taught by a successful voiceover actor and singer. I learned a lot and plan to pursue voiceover work eventually—either professionally or personally through my podcast. Either way, what happened after class is what gave me pause.

As I left the building, I noticed someone standing in the shadows—it was dark out. I wasn't too freaked out since other students were leaving, but when I realized it was Mel, I felt conflicted. It was very sweet of him, but I didn't understand why he was there. He said he was in the area and wanted to make sure I had arrived safely. It turned out to be a half-truth—he had wanted to make sure I got to class safely, so he made it a point to be in the area in order to find out.

Slowly, I started to think he might be insecure and trying to win me over. I couldn't understand why he was being so nice. I started to question whether he had ulterior motives or control issues. There's a popular dating term for when someone showers you with affection and attention early in a relationship: it's called "love bombing." Was that what he was doing?

I decided I would try to talk to him about it.

When I did, I totally failed. I called him and tried to explain how uneasy I felt about his actions. I wasn't trying to break up with him—I was just trying to express how I felt. It didn't go over well at all, and he ended our conversation by saying goodbye.

I was heartbroken. He seemed like such a good guy! I didn't know what to do, but I didn't want to let things end like that. I decided to text Mel's friend who ran the charity, since she was the only mutual contact I had, and explain what happened. I told her I wanted the chance to talk to him in person if he was willing—but if he wasn't, I still wanted him to understand what I was trying to say so he wouldn't repeat his actions with someone else going forward.

Fortunately, she stepped in and helped out. She asked him a very important question: "If your daughters were just starting to date someone and they did what you did, what would you think about it?" Put in that context, the lightbulb went off for him. He called me to apologize for overstepping boundaries. We talked for a while and agreed to meet again by taking a walk in a park.

I was nervous and excited as I waited for him to pick me up that day. I tried to distract myself, yet it was hard to think about anything else. When he showed up at my house, I didn't know how things would go. I was hopeful we could move past this, but what if he really thought things were over and was only trying to be polite by speaking to me in person?

Then, as Mel sat in my living room chair, he started to apologize for any misunderstanding. As he spoke, another phrase Angela B. had given me—*"Spirit, let me see what I need to see"*—suddenly popped into my head. And what I saw on his face was love. Just love. No ulterior motives. Mel's generosity is simply a part of who he is. He wasn't using it to gain affection or love from me, and he wasn't trying to manipulate me in any way. He is just a good man. Solid. He has a beautiful soul—and I needed to see it, because I had lost faith in finding a life partner.

Peace washed over me, and I started to feel his love back. It was amazing. I had never experienced that in a romantic relationship before. Our energies matched. Do you know how goddamn good that felt? If you're one of the lucky ones to have found someone who not only feels the same way about you as you do about them and shows it—then you've hit the jackpot. I believe my parents had that magic, and that's what I've always wanted.

Another great quality of Mel's is that he makes me feel safe—emotionally as well as physically. He is strong in strength, character, and personality, but he melts my heart with his kindness and his patience when it comes to working through problems. He has proven time and again to be a good listener and a good communicator. That is an invaluable aspect of a healthy relationship.

In fact, when we first started dating, Mel said to me that he wanted a relationship built on three things: *Respect, Appreciation, and Value.* He would give those things to me if I gave them to him. And he has made it very easy to do this—because he lives what he preaches.

I'm one lucky girl.

Let's get something straight. Having someone else in your life is a bonus—if that's what you want. But it shouldn't be a need. I say this because too often I've heard from both men and women that they don't like being lonely, and that's why they're looking for love.

Wait a second! Didn't I talk about this earlier?

My philosophy is that we should all start by enjoying our own company. Ultimately, we die alone—so to speak—so start acting like that's going to happen and get used to it. I don't mean the *dying* part, but the *being alone* part. If you don't like your own company, then you're in for trouble down the line.

And boys and girls, let's also remember this: don't expect him or her to be something they aren't. That isn't fair to either of you.

8

Mental Illness Versus Mental Health

I am not a physician who studied the brain, nor am I a doctor who studied the psyche. I can't even pretend to be a therapist, since I don't have a degree in social work. What I *can* do, however—as someone who has been a mental health patient—is offer a unique perspective on the difference between mental health and mental illness.

Many, many people confuse the two or think they're interchangeable. They are not. Simply put: we all have mental health. It's an essential part of our well-being. And sometimes, we run into issues that negatively affect it. Heck, country music practically thrives on songs full of life's downfalls and disappointments. A guy loses his girl, his truck breaks down, and his dog runs away. You know the drill. The song usually ends with him heading to a bar to commiserate with his buddies. And somehow, he gets over it—either because he has the emotional maturity to deal with his mess or because the check from his hit song softened the blow. (I'm just guessing here.)

Conversely, even happiness affects our mental health if you think about it. A few songs that, in my humble opinion, are total mood boosters: *Don't Worry, Be Happy, Walking on Sunshine,* and the aptly titled *Happy.* Listening to music is one of my favorite coping skills. A good song—especially an upbeat one—can completely flip my mood. Especially if I'm driving alone. No matter the genre, if it hits right, I'll crank the volume. Whether it's Led Zeppelin's *Immigrant Song,* Big Country's *In a Big Country* or Vivaldi's *The Four Seasons* (*Spring,* of course)—I'm in. And if either Phil Collins' *In the Air Tonight* or A Flock of Seagulls' *I Ran* comes on while I'm stopped at a light? You better believe I'm nailing those drum solos on my steering wheel and dashboard. It's just the way I roll.

REPEAT AFTER ME: It's when events that impact our mental health become so overwhelming that they start to permeate our lives—making it hard to function—that mental health crosses the line into *mental illness.*

Somewhere along my journey, I started to feel... different. I began to question my diagnosis of Bipolar 2 Disorder. My family never believed it, and some of my close friends didn't either. When they voiced their doubts, I felt insulted—like they were invalidating my feelings. It seemed dismissive, and it was discouraging. But eventually, things started to fall into place. And I began to wonder: *What if they're right?*

As luck (or fate) would have it, I had another therapist named Angela—Angela C.—assigned to me shortly after my back-to-back hospitalizations. She specializes in family crises and has worked with all kinds of patients and situations. She's really, *really* good at giving advice in a no-bullshit way—kind of like an iron fist in a velvet glove. She tells it like it is.

One day, she told me I was unlike many of her other patients. She meant it as a compliment. She praised my perseverance during dark times and said she admired my strength and willingness to keep searching for answers instead of giving up. I've always been stubborn, and I guess—when it's channeled well—that stubbornness can be a superpower.

Once Angela C. pointed that out, I began to notice differences between myself and the other patients I encountered in group therapy and support groups. I realized that, in my case, when someone offered a problem-solving suggestion—or I stumbled upon one myself—I would actually try it, as long as it seemed reasonable. I *always* try. In fact, I've told many people that I want "She tried" engraved on my tombstone.

Unfortunately, not everyone handles life that way. I started to see a pattern—people who would listen to advice, agree it was a good idea, and then either not follow through or just ignore it completely. Nine times out of ten, I think fear is the reason. And to be clear, I'm not fearless—I've said that before. I just know I don't want to die with regrets. That's what pushes me to try more often than not.

Still, something felt off. I knew I needed to explore a different avenue for help. Around that time, my daughter was also having difficulty with her emotions and communication. I suggested she see a therapist. She initially began working with a counselor due to extreme health anxiety. A doctor had mentioned that the anxiety—and the attention-seeking behavior surrounding it—might be tied to Borderline Personality Disorder (BPD).

But after a few sessions, her therapist disagreed. She didn't think it was BPD. Instead, she suggested my daughter might be on the Autism spectrum, like her brother. And suddenly, things started to click.

My daughter has been picked on and left out since she was little. Beginning in first grade, she struggled to make friends and was constantly excluded from playdates. It didn't help that she could be obstinate and blunt. I've often described her as the female version of Sheldon from *The Big Bang Theory*. She would absolutely knock on your door for hours until you opened it. (If you know, you know.) Still, like Sheldon, she has a big heart and is a truly good person.

So I started wondering—*was this it? Was she autistic?*

And what about me?

I've always felt like I struggle with verbal communication, especially when trying to clearly express a point. I also overreact when faced with confusing or difficult situations. Were these symptoms of mental illness... or signs I might be on the spectrum too?

When my daughter's therapist recommended an Autism evaluation for her, I decided to schedule one for myself as well. If both of my children had ASD, it had to come from somewhere, right?

At the same time, I was getting advice from a psychologist who specializes in BPD. I had reached out to him to learn better ways to parent my daughter. As with most first appointments, he asked a ton of questions—about her behavior, past diagnoses, and current challenges. When he asked if I ever felt like I was walking on eggshells around her, I answered honestly: that had only happened a few times.

After her therapist floated the Autism possibility, the psychologist agreed that my daughter probably didn't have BPD—she just didn't fit the profile. As for Autism? He wasn't sure. It wasn't his specialty.

One day, after we'd spoken a few times, the psychologist asked me to remind him why I had been hospitalized twice for suicidal thoughts. I explained that during my divorce, I had decided to go off an antidepressant I'd been taking for six years. I was advised to not taper it down but cut the dose in half. Shortly after doing that, I experienced extreme panic attacks, heart palpitations, and restless leg syndrome. I felt like I was either going to kill myself or be killed by the stress my body and mind were under. I checked myself into the hospital, and the staff there told me my symptoms were likely triggered by the medication.

He listened carefully, then hit me with this: he strongly believed I had been misdiagnosed.

What I'd experienced, he explained, sounded much more like withdrawal than a triggered episode. After all, if I actually had Bipolar Disorder—Type 1 or 2—I likely would've been triggered *before* that, not after taking that class of medication successfully for six years.

Then he gave me even better news: he believed my depression was situational, not conditional.

SHUT THE FRONT DOOR. WHAT? HOLY SHIT, BATMAN. That made so much more sense. I practically skipped out of his office that day.

My daughter and I waited several months for our psychological evaluations. It felt like an eternity waiting for the results. From childhood testing, we already knew she had low reasoning skills and ADHD. But what surprised us was a diagnosis we'd never heard of before: Social Pragmatic Communication Disorder (SPCD).

Basically, it summed up most of the issues she has relating to other people.

Here's the AI-generated definition (because you *know* I Googled it immediately):

"A developmental condition where individuals struggle to use verbal and nonverbal communication effectively in social situations, including difficulties understanding social cues, taking turns in conversation, adapting language to different contexts, and interpreting non-literal language, all while having relatively normal language skills in terms of grammar and vocabulary. Essentially, it's a problem with the 'social rules' of communication."

In real life? She's a blurter. She constantly interrupts me when I'm on the phone. It explained so much—why she's had trouble making and keeping friends, and why work environments are so challenging for her.

Also during the time of her psychological testing, her otolaryngologist diagnosed her with hearing loss. I'm convinced that's another huge factor in her communication struggles. I mean, can you imagine how lonely it must be to not fully understand what's happening around you?

I wish I could sprinkle fairy dust over her and make it all better. But she's 22 now. I can only do so much. She's going to have to learn how to adapt. And honestly, I have seen some improvement. As a kid, she had a strong aversion to basic manners. Now? She'll say "thank you"—even to me. Sometimes. On a Tuesday. When the weather is just right.

Then it was my turn. Time to find out what was going on inside my brain.

Lo and behold, the results came back and revealed that I was…

drumroll please…

an *ASSHOLE!*

At least that's how it felt. The tests showed I didn't have Autism. I didn't have ADHD (which I kind of expected). I didn't even have SPCD like my daughter. I was totally at a loss.

Why was verbal communication still so hard for me? Why did I feel like a good person but sometimes piss people off without meaning to? I mean, sure, there are a few people in this world I've pissed off on purpose, but I'd say it's more of an 80/20 thing. Just sayin'.

Also—why do I need things explained to me more than once? Why don't I get certain jokes, especially literal ones?

I had asked the doctor similar questions while going over my results and she brought up a really important point: I have very low Executive Function skills (EFS).

Turns out, so does my daughter.

What the heck does that mean? Let me explain. Many people confuse a lack of EFS with having ADHD. And while there's definitely some crossover, ADHD is a diagnosed neurological disorder, whereas low EFS is the result of lacking certain cognitive or intellectual skills—things like planning, prioritizing, organizing, and emotional self-regulation. In other words, my daughter and I are messy, we can't prioritize, and we tend to fly off the handle at the slightest provocation.

I know you're thinking, "Nan, you overreact to things?" To which I must honestly reply—have you counted the number of times I've used exclamation points throughout this writing?

Living together with these similarities for the last five years has been, well, difficult to say the least. At times, our emotions have escalated to a fever pitch—one of the main reasons my son chose to live with his dad. But through both family and individual therapy, we've learned to tone things down a bit. Still, as my daughter has so astutely pointed out, "Mom, a lot of times you and I are saying the same things. We're just saying it in two completely different ways." To which she added, "That's probably because you're 60 and I'm 22." She sure is wise.

Sure, I've talked a lot about therapy, testing, and diagnoses. That's because I'm one of those people who has to know the *why* before I take action. It's just how I'm wired. One foot in front of the other—that's generally how I go. And having the right tools to develop a plan helps me tame my dysfunctional Executive Functions. It's a win-win!

9

Mistakes I've Made and Advice for the Recently Single

I broke a mirror recently. They say that means seven years of bad luck. But you know what? I'll take whatever it indicates. I'm Iron Man in a dress now. Over these past five years, I've accomplished so many things I never thought I was capable of doing on my own. Aside from going through a divorce, it's well-known that buying a vehicle and purchasing real estate are two of the most stress-inducing events. I was fortunate to receive the marital home as part of my divorce settlement (kudos again to Ms. Diana Fredericks). And a year after the divorce was final, I had a discussion with my brother, Rich. I was managing the house and land, but it was becoming a burden. I asked him if he thought I should sell. He kindly told me he knew I was capable, but thought I should ask myself if I wanted to continue doing it. I didn't.

Looking back, the process of selling the home wasn't too painful. Or maybe—like childbirth—I'm forgetting. Either way, cleaning out a place

I'd lived in for more than 20 years with three other people and a few animals wasn't easy. But it got done, piece by piece, and I don't regret shedding another part of my former life. The house I thought I'd grow old in was now filled with too much negative energy. I was happy to let it go.

In its place, I ended up renting a loft with my daughter in an old factory converted into apartments. It had a cool, industrial vibe and reminded me of the Bronx, where I attended college. It was supposed to be my dream residence. Growing up in the New York City area, I'd see loft apartments in magazines like *Architectural Digest* and dream of living in something similar one day. I thought they were the epitome of glamour and sophistication. Unfortunately, my dream turned into a nightmare because the building owners never insulated the floors, and we could hear our neighbors below us every time they spoke. To make matters worse, the woman downstairs had this wonderful habit of screaming at her boyfriend regularly. Once, when I was sick, I politely texted to ask her if they could move their conversation to the living room because I could hear them while lying in bed. She refused to take accountability for any grievances and gave me a rather rude response about my own noise level. To be fair, I'm sure she heard my daughter and me as well— on occasion, but certainly not every day. Fed up with her banshee ways, I decided to repeat back to her exactly what their conversation was. She didn't respond. Unfortunately, that truce only lasted a day, and we moved out after a year of her torment. The previous occupants of the apartment had informed me afterward that her obscene noise level was their reason for leaving too.

That issue aside, living in the apartment complex was fun. I made a few friends, and since we were together during the pandemic, a group of us bonded and hosted get-togethers in each other's residences. We had Taco Tuesdays, International Night, and a Halloween costume party, to name a few. There were also bars and restaurants in the buildings that we could walk to, which helped us make the most of our lockdown. I'm sure it helped all of us stay sane during that crazy time.

When I was ready to find a new home, I turned to one of those neighbors, Michael, a real estate agent. He and his husband, Drew, were also looking to move. At first, I was on the fence about renting versus buying, and Michael accommodated me with viewings of both. But just as I was about to sign a lease on a new apartment, the listing for this charming little house popped up, and I asked Michael to see it immediately. The moment I walked in, I knew I would buy it. I was drawn straight from the front door to the sliding glass doors at the back of the house. There before me was a stunning view of trees and hills in the distance above the other houses. It faces northwest, and I swear I can see a slice of the Delaware Water Gap between the towering pines. I felt a rush and chills as I stood there. My parents came to mind. They are buried up in the Poconos, facing in the same direction. I believe they brought me there.

If you have the means to buy a piece of real estate, I strongly urge you to do it. It's truly empowering to own something that is strictly yours. Think about it: here in the United States, women were only given the right to their own mortgages in 1974. That was only 50 years ago! I can't imagine my mom not having that same right as I now do. We know we still have more to strive for.

Another good investment to have is a car. You can argue that cars rarely increase in value and depreciate the minute they leave the dealer's parking lot, but think of it as instant freedom. Having your own vehicle allows you to go anywhere, at any time. In the five years since my divorce, I've bought and sold one truck and four cars. I purchased the truck and one of the cars completely on my own, and it was quite nerve-wracking. I think I got good deals on each, but the whole au-to-buying process still feels shrouded in mystery.

I know it may sound excessive to have so many vehicles for just two people, but there were underlying circumstances with each. I love trucks, but I only had one for a year because it was too hard to park at the apartment complex, and it wasn't gas-efficient for my daughter to use for her commute to high school. I traded it for a smaller vehicle, but when my daughter abused the privilege of using that, I sold it with Mel's help. I think I only owned it for a few months. Today, she drives an 18-year-old SUV that's more appropriate for someone her age who works part-time. My own vehicle was totaled in an unfortunate acci-dent, and when it had to be replaced, I turned again to Mel and his best friend for advice. This time, I used the "Let me think about it" trick and walked away after negotiating with the salesman for over an hour. We were so close on the price, but I wanted just a little more taken off, and he wasn't budging. Leaving the showroom to get some lunch and then returning an hour later worked in my favor, and I got the price reduc-tion I wanted. It was another empowering moment, and I'm very proud of how I handled it.

Since I'm a big believer in finding solutions to problems and love passing on what I've learned, I've compiled a few suggestions I hope you'll find helpful. Sprinkled in with my own advice are some words of wisdom from friends who, like me, found themselves single in mid-life:

- **Rotate your tires every time you get your oil changed!** This one's huge for me because I went through two sets of tires within a year of being divorced. When I asked the tire center why this happened, they told me it wouldn't have happened if I had just rotated my tires regularly. While we were still married, L. may have mentioned this little nugget, but I had forgotten—it's a small detail with big consequences.

- **Draw up a Will!** Even if you don't think you have anything of value, you probably do. And despite its morbid nature, it's so important to be prepared. I strongly recommend putting together an Advanced Directive as well, so your loved ones know your wishes should something catastrophic happen. There are plenty of low-cost options to guide you through the process without an attorney, whether it's online or with a kit purchased at an office supply store.

- **Learn how to fix things!** My girlfriend, Sandee, made it a point to ask for help at home improvement stores when tackling a small repair or project. She suggests watching YouTube videos for tutorials as well.

- **Dress for yourself** and your girlfriends, not for a man! (Another gem from Sandee.)

- **Change the battery** in your thermostat before calling an HVAC company to unnecessarily check your furnace or heating system! This tip, from my girlfriend, Deb P., was learned the hard way when she could have made this simple change herself.

- **Be true to yourself!** This is another suggestion from Deb P., who is now a pickleball aficionado. Find something you like to do, with like-minded people, whether it's pickleball, game nights, or joining a book club. (Ooh, I have a book I can suggest!)

- **Find a support group!** My friend, Mary, recommended finding a group specifically for women going through similar circumstances. This gave her practical tools to move forward, along with genuine support from those who understood what she was going through.

- **Dress to impress when job hunting!** Mary also found a career closet where she could get professional clothing for interviews. In addition to the nationwide nonprofit Dress for Success, you can likely find other local options in your area as well.

- **Seek solace!** Finding a place of worship can be instrumental in divorce recovery. Mary feels that joining a church provided another layer to her healing.

- **Move forward!** Letting go of resentment toward your ex-spouse brings peace, as Mary and I both discussed. This has taken me some time, but as Elsa sings in Let It Go," *It's funny how some distance makes everything seem small.* I can honestly say this is true for me. The space between 2018 and now has given me the time to move on with grace. I wish the same for L. too.

10

You Don't Know What You Don't Know

I purchased my first set of hearing aids the other day. Years ago, I was told I had some hearing loss, but I chose to ignore it because I felt it was more of an annoyance to wear them than a necessity to correct my hearing. When I finished this most recent test, the auditory specialist suggested I try on a pair to see if I noticed a difference. I did. Although my voice was loud and tinny (I was told that was due to the volume being turned up too high on my end), everyone else's was much richer. It was a very weird sensation.

When I conveyed this to the gentleman helping me, he suggested I probably had this hearing issue for longer than I knew and may have experienced auditory deprivation. Of course, I had to look that up! And when I did, it seemed to make more than just my hearing clear. It's a condition in which the brain doesn't receive enough stimulation to activate neurons in the auditory cortex. What does this mean? Well, it's like this: you can say something to me, and if I hear you clearly, then I will hopefully understand what you are saying and be able to respond back. But if I can't hear what you are saying clearly, then I may jump to conclusions, or, as is often the case, have to ask for things to be repeated. When that happens, you lose something. It's like trying to see through cheesecloth; you can see outlines, but you don't get the whole picture. In other words, it slows down your processing because this lack of neuron firing forces you to lose your place in conversations. If it happens consistently, over time it becomes draining and is a huge contributor to poor communication skills. Of course, this can lead to other skill deficits too. Like poor Executive Functions.

As I mentioned earlier, my daughter also has hearing loss and now wears hearing aids. Since we only discovered the deficiency recently, I strongly believe it contributed to her social communication difficulties. I can't go back in time, but if we had known she was dealing with this issue earlier in her life, it would have made things a bit easier for her. Maybe not golden, but I'm sure there would have been some benefits to having tools and resources that could have guided her to a better social life. It enrages me that so many professionals who crossed her path—whether educationally, medically, or casually—never once suspected anything was wrong, despite my pleas for help. What they saw, as L. and I did, was an obstinate and defiant child. Although most approached her with kindness and compassion, there were plenty of dismissive attitudes about her growing out of this, whatever "it" was. But my motherly instinct suspected there was more to this situation, and I did the best I could by advocating for the support she needed. But deep in my heart, I wish I could have given her a better childhood.

As for me, I obviously coped with my social and academic situations differently as a child, whether I had been experiencing the loss sooner in life as well. Since we didn't have educational plans back then, like 504s or IEPs, my mom just put me in remedial classes and hoped for the best. Socially, I had a multitude of brothers and sisters to imitate (whether good or bad), so I managed to blend in as they did. But when I got older and entered college, I decided to embrace my "weirdness." It was the height of the Punk and New Wave movements, and I felt like I finally found how to fit in by gobbling up the music and fashion. I still had to work on my self-esteem, but once my skin finally cleared up, that boosted my confidence. The '80s were the best years for me.

In addition to my hearing loss and my daughter's, my father became profoundly deaf before passing away at the age of 86. Just like Asperger's, I believe there is a strong genetic connection to this condition we share. It's more than a mere coincidence. And thinking about how this affects communication and relationships, I want to share the reason why I chose the phrase, "You don't know what you don't know" as the title for this chapter.

This goes back to when I was married. L. works in sales where he receives compensation for expenses related to his work. So, his gas mileage, meals, hotel stays, office supplies, and training, for example, were covered by his company since he worked from home. This was pre-Covid, and his company's headquarters were in California. Very often, he became overwhelmed by filling out the paperwork for reimbursement and would angrily express his frustration. He also dragged his feet on getting the task done because it was time-consuming, and then he would be upset with himself for not getting the money back in a timely manner. From what I remember, his office would send him frequent reminders. I'm sure they wanted to get it off their books and were probably just as frustrated with him.

Anyway, being the dutiful wife and stay-at-home mom, I foolishly offered to take on that responsibility for him. After all, I was already handling our taxes, homeowners, car, and health insurance, managing the household, and raising our children, so what was one more administrative task to do? He appreciated the offer and took me up on it. He showed me how to input the information, and I went about gathering his receipts and materials. I did this for several months until one day when the administrative assistant at the home office called to tell him that his expenses were submitted incorrectly, and he wouldn't get paid for them unless the mistake was corrected. This meant he would have to wait again for his payment.

Well, of course, the issue was my fault because I should have known it was entered incorrectly, right? Think again. There was a step in the process he had neglected or forgotten to teach me, and when I pointed that out to him, he wouldn't let it go. He even replied that, because I took on the responsibility of helping him, I should have asked about it. To which I replied, "How would I have even known to ask about it when I didn't even know it was a thing?" As always, he refused to accept the accountability of being wrong. So, I went on to tell him he should be grateful I had volunteered to help in the first place, and that I would no longer be submitting his expenses for him.

The story of that argument fits here because it sums up how I was beginning to understand the frustration I had my whole life with communicating my thoughts and feelings to others. I knew I was right in that situation, yet my ex wouldn't admit I was. And that made me question myself, which made me not only angry with him but disappointed with myself. I grew angrier and more frustrated because I couldn't find the words to tell him how he upset me, so I just decided to stop helping him. I hated to do that because I really like to contribute when I can, but as it is with my Achilles heel, I would shut down when I couldn't figure out how to resolve a conflict. It was the snow globe effect once again—my feelings were all bottled up inside, and I couldn't figure out a healthy way to let them out.

11

And In the End

I'm really super good at owning my shit and can say unequivocally that I was not in love with my husband when he told me he wanted to leave me for another woman. When the pain from the ending of our relationship wore off, I discovered a great sense of relief because, for years, I had wanted to get out; I just didn't know how.

The bottom line is this: my ex-husband absolutely humiliated me during our divorce, but he didn't destroy me. And you know what I got in return? HAPPINESS. Real, unadulterated happiness. The kind other people talk about!

Remember, there will be good and bad days. That's life. There will probably be some really, really dark days. My worst day ever was when my son said he didn't want to celebrate Christmas with me for the first time and then subsequently moved out. That was worse than his father saying he wanted a divorce, and worse than committing myself to the hospital. I respect his decision now, but it was and still is very hard to let go of him. After all, how do you detach from the people you love? I felt I had failed him as his mom. He hasn't spoken to me much since then. I hold out hope that it will change one day. In the meantime, a friend and I are in the process of developing a support group for parents of estranged adult children. This is another subject for which I am passionate about breaking the stigma surrounding it.

As things started to unravel with L., the family therapist he and I had been seeing, Dan, imparted some very wise words to me. The day after I slapped my soon-to-be ex, we had a joint counseling session. When the cartoon meme situation came up, the therapist asked L. if he realized how awful that would make me feel, and his response was a baffling, "No, I had no idea." The counselor shot me an incredulous look. I wasn't particularly shocked, given his perpetual mistreatment. When pressed further that his antics of carrying on an affair while living under the same roof were disrespectful and hurtful, he stood up, bellowed something about where we lived being a "No-fault divorce state!" and stormed out. Yes, that was his response. He immediately called his lawyer, who advised him to file a police report about the slap in retaliation for upsetting him.

Yes, I was "arrested." But as with my hospital stay, it was nothing like you would have imagined. And prior to that incident, I would also not have imagined what being a perp would be like either. I was called down to our local State Troopers' barracks and asked to write out my side of the story. I did and then sat in their waiting room for quite some time. I was not told exactly what was going on until the "arresting" officer came back out to the lobby and explained that he had been on the phone with the D.A.'s office and that they had come to an agreement that I shouldn't be charged with a felony for assault and battery. EXCUSE ME, WHAAAAAT? I didn't realize a slap was that serious. However, I got it. I completely understood the law and realized how much their discussion worked in my favor, especially when the Trooper made the lighthearted remark that they knew I couldn't have done much damage after they met L. and me separately. Our sizes didn't come close. If the roles had been reversed, though, my ex would not have been in the same situation, because I'm sure it would have been worse for him. Although he did try to make it worse for me, ultimately. I read his report, and he claimed I punched him, which I did not. I would have broken my hand if I had. It was clearly open-handed, albeit with rings on, which could have been why it felt harder. I know hitting someone is not cool – even when it's damn deserved and feels so good. Either way, I was extremely grateful for the officer working on my behalf to lower the charge to a misdemeanor. The only thing was, now I had to appear in court to plead guilty and have the judge sentence me to probation. Like a good girl, I also had to promise not to do it again. Should I mention I had my fingers crossed behind my back while agreeing to the judge's admonishment? No? Okay, then I won't admit to it.

But before all of that happened, our therapist, Dan, said something profound I will never forget. After L. had stomped away from the last session and was peeling out of the parking lot in his car, Dan turned to me and said, "This could be the greatest gift you've ever received." And by the Holy Spirit, he was right! He also added, "Believe, just a little, that what you're going through right now is a valuable part of your life and that an overall benevolent process is taking place." Amen, amen, amen.

There you have it. My story from around the bend and back again.

Now it's your turn. I hope you have learned from my little tale that there is no right or wrong way to repair your life. Well, drinking or inhaling substances isn't going to help, but aside from that, you must decide how you are going to move forward. What are you doing to improve how you feel? What are you doing to improve your situation? Think about it and get back to me.

In conclusion, here's my advice to you, dear friend: Give life a chance to happen. You never know what to expect. And that's a beautiful thing. Don't squash your dreams because of 'what-ifs.' The 'what-ifs' will take care of themselves. Now grab your big girl panties, pull them up, and get out there. The world is waiting to hear from you, too! I know I am.

With much love, hugs, and kisses,

Nan

Epilogue

O nce, I had the good fortune of meeting the author, Elizabeth Gilbert — or Liz, as she likes to be called. She is genuine, kind, and warm. You can tell she is sincerely interested in people and hearing their stories. The occasion was a very small fundraising event for my friend, Michelle, who was launching a nonprofit. Her goal was to raise enough money to provide free haircuts to homeless and battered women in our local area. As a hairstylist, Michelle knew the confidence a good haircut could give anyone. Liz had decided to join the event unannounced to introduce her dear friend, who later became her girlfriend, Rayya Ellis, as one of the speakers on the guest panel. Rayya was a kickass storyteller in her own right. If you ever get the chance, please read her memoir *Harley Loco*, which chronicles her journey from a child in the Middle East to her upbringing in America. She speaks frankly about her battles with addiction and overcoming them. Unfortunately, Rayya passed away from cancer at the tender age of 57.

After the panelists spoke, there was a cocktail party, and I managed to grab Liz's ear for a short conversation. I had a silly question to ask her, and she was gracious enough to listen to my tale in which I had mistaken someone else for her. The encounter with the mystery woman was prior to Liz's fame from the book and subsequent film *Eat, Pray, Love*. For years, I had thought I had given Liz a ride home from a mechanic whose service station was in our shared hometown area. It turns out it was not her, but another tall, blonde woman with a husky voice, and we had a good chuckle over my error.

She then asked me a really interesting question. Liz said, "Nancy, do you know what your ikigai (ee-kee-guy) is?" She went on to explain that this is the Japanese concept for defining your life's meaning by thinking about what you can contribute to the world through your talents, passions, and/or profession. It can be fluid because, over time, your ideas about what you love, what you're good at, what the world needs, or what you can be paid for can change. And some people believe finding your sense of purpose can lead to a more fulfilling, and possibly, longer life.

At the time Liz asked me that question, I didn't have an answer. I'm sure I sputtered out something of no significance, but I was dumbfounded to even venture a guess. Truth be told, I have struggled with why I was put on this earth for years, and it has haunted me ever since she asked me to define it. Was I a mom? Was I a writer? I had thought I was going to be both of those things, including a wife. And now, that was taken from me. As I lost my confidence in myself, I lost my confidence in what I could do.

Lately, though, I'm beginning to see what exactly my *ikigai* is. I'll give you a few examples. One weekend morning, Mel and I were having brunch at one of our favorite restaurants. As we were waiting for our waiter to take our order, we noticed an older woman standing near us, and she looked confused. She had taken a seat, and then, after a few minutes, got up but then hesitantly stood next to the table without leaving. We decided to ask her if she needed help. She responded that she was undecided as to whether she should stay to eat or not. Realizing she was alone, we both asked if she wanted to join us. And she did. We learned her name and that she had been a long-time resident of the area. She belonged to a local church, had a brother who lived nearby, but lived alone. I think she had been married, but I can't remember if she had any children.

Either way, we had a nice time chatting with her and sharing a meal. Well, Mel shared most of his because that's the way he is! We all smiled and laughed as we spent the time together. I am sure she was happy she decided to stay. We certainly were glad she did. It was a joy to do that for a stranger. But afterwards, I started crying as we left the restaurant. When Mel asked me what was wrong, I told him this was exactly the way I wanted to live my life. I wanted to just be a good person and help others whenever I could. Nothing more. He understood what I meant because he feels the same and tries to live his life like that.

On another occasion, I took a 5-hour round trip one day to sit with one of my dearest friends as she was going through a divorce and need-ed help figuring out how to get medical, car, and home insurance. Since I had already gone through this same experience a few years earlier, I was able to sit with her and guide her as she made the phone calls and filled out paperwork to start the process. By doing the work together, I felt like she had gained back some confidence many of us seem to lose when we end our relationships. As I left her home, I realized helping her in such a small way made me really happy, for both of us.

You know, I had wanted to live life like this when I was married to L., but he didn't understand my need to help others. He had been a member of his hometown Rescue Squad, so I automatically assumed he had the desire to be of service. I was mistaken. When I asked him why he joined, he told me it was to make his resume look better when he was job hunting. Clearly, we were not on the same page here as well. So, I stifled that part of myself because I felt inhibited from being the true person I was meant to be.

Therefore, Liz, if we ever get the chance to meet again and you ask me now what my ikigai is, I will proudly answer thus: It is, simply, to love. That's it. Just like my mom, I was put on this earth to provide love and comfort to those whose lives are intertwined with mine. It's that simple. I won't make money off of this way of life, which is fine. Because for now, it's enough.

I am finally me and I am finally free.

Resources

I have described at length how I had a lot of support on my journey to healing, and I'd like to help you find that assistance too. Listed here are a few of the organizations I received information from, and groups I attended. But if you or anyone close to you is experiencing suicidal thoughts or intentions, please call 9-1-1 first or go to your nearest Emergency Room. You can also call 9-8-8, the Suicide and Crisis Lifeline, to speak to someone 24 hours a day, seven days a week, and 365 days a year.

NAMI – The National Alliance on Mental Illness is the United States' largest grassroots mental health organization, with more than 700 chapters providing education and support in their local communities. You can find help by visiting their website: www.nami.org. In addition, if you or a loved one are struggling with mental health issues, you can call the NAMI HelpLine to connect with a volunteer for support. Available Monday through Friday, 10 AM – 10 PM EST, call 800-950-NAMI (6264), text "HelpLine" to 62640, or email them at helpline@nami.org.

CoDA – Codependents Anonymous is a 12-step program structured similarly to Alcoholics Anonymous. Their website is: www.coda.org. I am often asked, "What exactly IS codependence?" Or get comments like, "Aren't we all co-dependent?" In the words of the organization's website, I offer this description: What is codependence? Somewhere along the line, we learned to doubt our perception, discount our feelings, and overlook our needs. We looked to others to tell us what to think, feel, and how to behave. Other people supplied us with information about who we were and how we should be. It became more important to be compliant or avoidant rather than to be authentic, and we adopted rigid beliefs about what "should be." We believed that if we could just, "get it right," things would be okay. When we "got it wrong," our sense of security and self-worth evaporated. I totally relate to the avoidant rather than authentic persona. That is exactly what happened to me as I grew unhappy with my marriage.

DBSA – Depression, Bipolar Support Alliance. This organization's vision is to envision wellness for people living with mood disorders, and its mission is to provide hope, help, support, and education to improve the lives of people who have those disorders. Visit their website, www.dbsalliance.org to find a local chapter for group meetings. Since COVID, they have also implemented Zoom meetings. These have proven to be quite popular for days when depression makes it a struggle to even get out of bed.

Local Mental Health Board – Not every community has one, but my county did, and I volunteered for mine after leaving the hospital. It was really eye-opening to learn what resources are and aren't available to the population of underserved mental health patients. But it was fulfilling to be able to participate in the process of developing plans to help move the issues forward or just resolving issues that impeded progress.

And since I am such a strong supporter of therapy, I highly recommend you find one for yourself. Most insurance companies pay for these services now. I have said time and again that the good ones are like girlfriends you pay to listen to your sorrows! At least that's how I feel about my current psychotherapist, Ashley, who is super smart. To begin your search, go to Psychology Today's website, www.psychologytoday. com to find one in your area. Along with a picture and description of the counselor, you will also find their specialties listed.

If you find it difficult to meet with someone in person, there are online therapy companies to consider. Here are a few:

BetterHelp: betterhelp.com

Talkspace: talkspace.com

Talkiatry: talkiatry.com

Brightside: brightside.com

Teledoc: teledochealth.com

["Being able to be your true self is one of the strongest components of good mental health."]

Lauren Fogel Mersy, N.D.

Acknowledgments

I've had friends over the years, both casual and close. But it wasn't until I started writing this book that I discovered how important having a community is. I think it is a big part of what is missing in the world today, and I am doing my best to cultivate it in my own little corner. Therefore, I have many people in my community to thank for helping me with this book.

It all started with my two former Reader's Digest General Books colleagues, **Fred DuBose,** and **James McInnis.** Telling me to write down the details of my life these past five years was the best advice, Fred. And James, you helped get this project off the ground and your critique of my manuscript was (actually) constructive. I am grateful you two are still in my life after all these years.

Another pair instrumental in helping me start this project were **Kat Dixon** and **Lauren Green.** You both saw something in me I didn't yet know was there. Thank you for encouraging me to get things started and keep it going.

To my coach, **Iky Chan,** thank you for making me realize my dreams were possible to achieve! Your advice and support are paramount to my success. I am extremely grateful for our friendship and your continued dedication to me.

And to my podcast friends, **Steph Thompson,** and *John Chao,* thank you also for your continued guidance and encouragement in pursuing this project, the podcasts, and my spirituality. We may be scattered around the world, but you both have come together in my heart.

As for the **Silk Mill Gang** and **the Boys of the Silk Mill,** thank you for the laughter and friendship. I didn't know I needed a community until I moved into B312 and met all of you. Life is sweeter now because of it, and the times we've spent together helped in my healing process.

There are too many women I love to name here individually. Some made it into this book, but many didn't. However, whether we met during high school, college, work, my marriage, Irish Dance, or after my divorce, thank you all for sharing your stories, your tears, laughter, and advice. It is lovely to have developed such precious friendships. You all mean the world to me.

There are three women, however, who do get a special shout out. First, my therapists, **Ashley, and Angela C..** I am grateful to be your client but consider you my friends. You are both so smart and wise and have given me great advice over the years, most of which I follow! And to **Cheryl Covello** - I don't think we would have survived the *Purnell School* without each other. Thank you for the laughter, shoulder to cry on, and free legal advice. We are both good mothers, despite what we think of ourselves at times.

Thank you also to my siblings, **Diane, Tom, Rich, Jane, and George.** This will come as no surprise after today, but Mom and Dad really did consider me their favorite. Sorry I had to tell you this way, but I still love you all very, very much. I can't imagine life without being a part of our great family, and thanks for making life fun. At least now it is! And thank you to my sisters- and brothers-in law, **Babs, Sarah, Denis,** and **Clyde.** Your continued love and support mean the world to me. And to my soul sister, **Kathleen,** for always being there for me. The world is a better place with you in it.

I would be remiss if I didn't extend a heartfelt thank you to my publisher, **Jodi Costa** of **Shine Press.** Jodi, you've made this first-time author feel confident and at ease, knowing my book is in the capable hands of you and your team. My journey with you has been both fun and educational, and I eagerly anticipate future collaborations. You truly chose the perfect name for your company, because you shine brightly as a cheerleader for all your clients!

I'd also like to thank those family and friends who have remained in my life and my kids' lives after the divorce. You have shown us so much grace. I am truly grateful for our continued relationships.

Finally, to the man of my heart, **Mel Lawson,** I am honored to be spending the rest of my life with you. You make our time together so much easier, richer, and just damn fun! I can't wait to see what the future holds for us. We are very lucky to have found each other. And like our song, *Something Just Like This,* we don't have superhuman gifts, but we do turn to each other again and again with respect, appreciation, and value. Thank you for listening to me with your heart and loving me as perfectly as you do.

Connect with the Author

Website: NanBerrian.com

Building Bridges Info: NanBerrian.com/estrangement

About the Author

If someone had told young Nancy "Nan" Berrian she'd one day become a professional writer, she would have laughed—and honestly, she still finds it a bit surprising. Her journey began in 7th grade, when her English teacher, Mrs. Restaino, held up Nan's synopses of *The Cherry Orchard* and *A Doll House* as classroom examples. As a student who had quietly struggled in school, that recognition lit a spark.

Despite undiagnosed learning challenges—or perhaps because of them—Nan pursued a career in communications, spending many years writing for others in the corporate world. But she always held on to the dream of expressing herself through her own words. With her debut book, *Vows, Wows, and WTF?!*, she's finally doing just that—and like Grandma Moses, she's glad she started before it was too late.

Nan lives in Pennsylvania's picturesque Lehigh Valley with her daughter, their beloved three-legged rescue pup, and a mischievous cat. Recently she became the co-founder of a support group for families of estranged children and siblings, the only one available in the Valley. She enjoys concerts and the local arts scene with her partner, Mel, and treasures time spent with her large and loving extended family.

www.ingramcontent.com/pod-product-compliance
Lightning Source LLC
Chambersburg PA
CBHW070336130626
46556CB00007B/2882